I0142250

wo*me*n

women

Aging Healthfully, Beautifully, and Gracefully

Body, Soul, and Spirit

DEBORAH W. MORRISON

women: Aging Healthfully, Beautifully, and Gracefully; Body, Soul, and Spirit

Copyright © 2021 by Deborah W. Morrison. All rights reserved.

No part of this publication may be reproduced, stored in a retrieval system or transmitted in any way by any means, electronic, mechanical, photocopy recording or otherwise without the prior permission of the author except as provided by USA copyright law.

Scripture quotations marked (NIV) are taken from the Holy Bible, New International Version ®, Copyright © 1973, 1978, 1984 by International Bible Society. Used by permission of Zondervan Publishing House. All rights reserved.

Scripture quotations marked (NLT) are taken from the Holy Bible, New Living Translation, copyright © 1996, 2004, 2007. Used by permission of Tyndale House Publishers, Inc. Carol Stream, Illinois 60188. All rights reserved.

Cover and interior design by Elite Authors

Published in the United States of America

ISBN: 978-1-7370114-0-8

www.greaterisjesusinme.com

Dedication

I dedicate this book in loving memory of Mrs. Hyacinth (Inez) Alexandra Wilson McDonald, my mom. She's my inspiration, my sHERO! She was beautiful, classy, elegant, savvy, talented, artistic, creative, resourceful, jack-of-all-trades and, a strong and fearless woman.

My father, Stanley C. Wilson, was the breadwinner, as we'd say back in the day, and he made sure we had what we needed. Ma was a housewife, and she took care of everything else. She took excellent care of her husband and her seven children. She did it all!

Above all, Ma was a woman of God, filled with Godly wisdom and counsel, and a prayer warrior. Ma lived her life to love, honor, and glorify God. She loved serving God and taking care of His people. That's why today I'm a Christ-filled, spirit-led woman, just like Ma. I'm honored and humbled to follow in her footsteps and carry her torch. I'm so thankful to my Heavenly Father for blessing me in this very special way.

"She is clothed with strength and dignity, and she laughs without fear of the future.When she speaks her words are wise, and she gives instructions with kindness. She carefully watches everything in her household and suffers nothing from laziness. Her children stand and bless her. Her husband praises her:There are many virtuous and capable women in the world, but you surpass them all. Charm is deceptive, and beauty does not last; but a woman who fears the Lord will be greatly praised. Reward her for all she has done. Let her deeds publicly declare her praise."

Proverbs 31:25-31 (NLT)

Ma was my first love. I love her so much! I've always said the umbilical cord was never cut. She is my role model. She introduced me to God, Jesus, and Holy Spirit, and that's the best gift she could have ever given me. I'll cherish this gift forever.

Ma was my beauty role model. From an early age she taught me to love and take care of myself. Skincare was extremely important to her. Ma had me when she was 45 years old. I am the last of seven children. So, when I really started noticing the things she was doing, she was in her late fifties, around my age.

I remember watching Ma apply Oil of Olay moisturizer religiously on her face; she believed in it. She would place five small dollops on her face (one on her forehead, one on the tip of her nose, one on each cheek, and one on her chin).When spreading the moisturizer on her cheeks she would move her hands in upward strokes and say "push up." She believed this helped keep that area from sagging.

Dry skin runs in my mom's family; therefore, she was very conscious about it and was always looking for products that would keep our skins hydrated and moisturized. I remember seeing her make coconut oil from scratch. We'd use it on our whole bodies, from scalp to toe. As we know, coconut oil has many benefits and it really helped us.

Years later, Ma mixed Pond's Cold Cream and Vaseline Petroleum Jelly, and that's what we used on our skins. As an adult, I continued using this mixture and added a few drops of pure glycerin oil. Then when I moved to the U.S., I replaced the glycerin oil with baby oil until I found the dry skin miracle lotion, Curél. Let me tell you, Curél is the best lotion that ever happened to my skin. I've been using it for over 20 years, and it is still effective and still delivers the same great results. We'll talk more about Curél later on.

Ma never left home without makeup. She'd put on foundation, powder, black eyebrow pencil, red blush and red lipstick. She loved her red lipstick! She never went to a beauty salon. She did everything for herself, i.e., straightened her hair with hot comb when she wasn't wearing it natural, cut and colored her hair black leaving a gray patch, and did her own manicure and pedicure. Ma was meticulous, detailed, making sure she did everything right. I watched her do it all! And she taught me to do things for myself.

Ma designed and sewed her own clothes and her daughters' clothes too and they fit perfectly and looked great. We all got compliments all the time. My mom would tell me that for your clothes to look right on you, you had to wear the right undergarments, i.e., a good fitting bra and girdle (in those days). I never wore a girdle, but I did wear tummy control panties that really helped me after I had my son. That helped my tummy area get back in shape in no time.

She also told me to hang my clothes properly on the hanger because however it hung on the hanger, it would hang on you. So till today, I make sure my clothes are hung properly on hangers.

Ma believed in poise and proper posture. She believed a woman should carry herself with dignity, decency, grace, class, and elegance. She'd say, "Lift up your head. Smile! Stand tall. Walk tall." At a young age, she had me put a phone book on my head, look forward, not down and walk in a straight line. She'd have me stand at an angle, shoulders back and put one foot in front of the other. She taught me how to walk, stand, and sit gracefully. I still do all those things because they were deep rooted in me, so they come naturally.

Ma would always say to me, "There is a right way and a wrong way to do things. Do it the right way the first time, then you won't have to do it again." It wasn't about doing things perfect, it was about doing things the right way, with excellence.

Ma was gifted and talented in so many ways. She played the violin, drew, made floral arrangements, crocheted dresses/hats, was a handy woman around the house, a cook, baker, seamstress, church leader, public speaker, organizer, prayer warrior, etc. and filled with good old common sense. She'd say, "Common sense beats all senses."

I'll be honest, when Ma was raising me, imparting wisdom, teaching and grooming me into the woman I am today (which I didn't know that's what she was doing at that time), most of the times I was not happy or receptive or appreciative about any of it. But I was listening, thank God. Today I remember all those things and value and appreciate every one of them. I'm grateful and thankful to Ma for teaching me, not giving up on me, and for all she did for me. All the things I learned from her are priceless and I will cherish them forever. It all makes sense now! I miss my mother and she lives in my heart forever.

I'm also grateful and thankful to Ma for instilling in me self-love, self-acceptance, self-know/worth, self-care, self-confidence, self-esteem, and self-discipline. I grew up knowing who I am. I knew that nobody was better than me and I was not better than anybody. She taught me decency and to treat everybody with dignity and respect and to not accept anything less from anyone. She taught me to have values, standards, set boundaries and not accept everything and anything. Not to settle for less and always strive for better.

Ma didn't need anyone to tell her she was beautiful or needed validation, she knew it because she knew she was God's daughter. She knew she was fearfully and wonderfully made by her Heavenly Father. And she raised me to know that I am beautiful no matter what anyone thinks or says because I'm God's daughter. I'm fearfully and wonderfully made by my Heavenly Father. Ma, I love you and thank you for the strong foundation.

- Who is your sHERO? Is it your mom, aunt, older sister, cousin, teacher, coach, mentor, older friend? You might have more than one sHERO. That's all good! I have always had older women in my life, my older sisters and friends, sharing their wealth of knowledge with me and giving good counsel, and keeping me grounded, straight, and levelheaded. It takes a village of strong women to raise a strong woman.

- What have you learned from your sHERO? What are the memories you cherish the most? If she is still alive, have you reached out to her lately and thanked her? Have you told her how much you love and appreciate her? If you haven't, stop reading and call (rather than text) or text (if you can't call) your sHERO and tell her how you feel about her. And visit often, if possible. When I became an adult and realized all what my mom did for me, I made sure to take every opportunity I had to thank her and tell her how much I loved her and appreciated everything she taught me and did for me. My sHERO!

- Or you might well be someone's sHERO. You go girl!

Contents

TOTAL BODY CARE

HEALTH CARE

Introduction

Hi, dear! I know you want to be the best you, want the best for you and want to live your best life. We all do.

But before we get into the nitty-gritty of this I book, I want you to know that you are the reason I wrote this book. Yes, you! Because sharing is caring (I got this phrase from Willie, my co-worker). And I care for you. I know what you're thinking… "You don't know me, so how can you care for me?" Well, I don't have to know you to care for you, and pray for you. God knows you! That's what matters.

I want to inspire, encourage and empower women to be their best version at any age. I want to encourage you to love, know, accept and take the best care of the body God gave you. It's the only one you have. You know that, right? My tips will help you to look your best in your body, feel comfortable in it, age healthfully, beautifully, and gracefully in it, live a longer life, and keep the wrinkles away for a long time. I know this is what you want for yourself.

I'm so excited for you! I'll be sharing with you my best beauty and total body care tips—from head to toe—and the affordable products I use. You and I will be talking about everything—and I mean everything.

We will talk about those things we don't normally talk about or feel uncomfortable talking about. In some instances, you might even think, No she didn't. Ahh, yes, I did! Because someone has to talk about it. Just keeping it real! The good news is, it's between you and me.

We will also talk about your soul and spirit because they are important and they matter to God. Your body is God's temple, and your soul (who you are) and your spirit (your connection to God) live in it. Your soul and spirit play an important role in the way you live your life, the way you feel about yourself and others, and the way you treat yourself and others. Above all, they play an important role in the way you feel about God, Jesus and the Holy Spirit and your relationship with Them. This is why you want your soul and spirit to be healthy, beautiful and graceful.

One thing I know is that when you're done reading this book, you will want to make the most and get the most out of you: body, soul and spirit. You will desire to be the best you and live your best life here and now to be continued in heaven. Are you ready? Let's do this together!

But before we jump into it, please allow me to pray for you.

Let's pray…

God our Father, bless this phenomenal woman abundantly in every area of her life. Give her what she needs, when she needs it and give her the desires of her heart. Fill her with Your wisdom and discernment, and guide her through her life. Equip her with everything she needs to succeed in everything she does. Let her rise and shine every day! And let her feel Your divine presence, love and comfort. Fill her heart with Your love, peace, joy and hope. Keep her safe and protected at all times.

Thank You Lord for all the great things You have done for her, in her and through her, and the great things You will continue to do for her, in her and through her.

Heavenly Father, let her know her worth. Let her know her greatness, and appreciate and value all the great things you have put in her. Use her to do Your work and to bless others with the gifts you have given her, for Your honor and glory.

Almighty God, I lift up Your precious daughter to You, in the mighty name of our Lord and Savior Jesus Christ. Amen

"And I am certain that God, who began the good work within you, will continue his work until it is finally finished on the day when Christ Jesus returns."

Philippians 1:6 (NLT)

"Now may the God of peace make you holy in every way, and may your whole spirit and soul and body be kept blameless until our Lord Jesus Christ comes again."

1 Thessalonians 5:23 (NLT)

"Dear friend, I hope all is well with you and that you are as healthy in your body as you are strong in spirit."

3 John 1:2 (NLT)

Let's get started!

Your Body, Soul, And Spirit

Your Body is God's Temple

Did you know that your body is God's temple? It sure is! This is the one and only body God gave you and it is His temple. Woo hoo!

You know what? Sometimes you just have to take time to reflect on things you don't think about often or at all because you take them for granted. This is one of those things and times. What I'd like you to do right now is to reflect on this: Your body is God's temple. Let that truth sink in for a minute.

Yes, your body is God's temple! It is precious and should be much appreciated and valued by you and everyone else and treated with the utmost tender, loving, care (TLC). So, have you ever thought of your body as God's temple? How do you feel about this?

This is what I'd like you to do. Go to your mirror and take a good look at yourself. Take it all in. Oh yes! You are looking at God's temple. YOU! The same way you are in awe when you see all of God's wonderful creations and want to take it all in, that's the same way you should be in awe when you see yourself in the mirror. You are God's wonderful creation. You are too awesome!

This is exactly why you should want to love, know, accept, and take the best care of your precious body, God's temple. And your soul and your spirit live in God's temple. Too wonderful!

It is time to make the most and get the most out of your body. To my younger lady, it is never too early to start. To my older lady, it is not too late to start. Let's get right to it!

"Don't you realize that your body is the temple of the Holy Spirit, who lives in you and was given to you by God? You do not belong to yourself, for God bought you with a high price. So you must honor God with your body."

1 Corinthians 6:19-20 (NLT)

God Gave You One Body

$$\sim \!\!\!\sim \!\!\! \bigcirc \!\!\! \bigcirc \!\!\! \sim$$

A s I mentioned before, God gave you one body. You can't exchange it, trade it in, give it away or use someone else's body. You're going to live in your body for the rest of your life, till death do you part. Oh yes! Until you're absent from the body and present with the Lord (2 Corinthians 5:8). So why not make the most and get the most out of it?

How do you feel about your body? Are you happy with it? Do you feel good and comfortable in it? Is your body healthy? Are you aging beautifully and gracefully in it? Do you love, know, accept and take the best care of your body?

The reason I ask these questions is because over the years I've met women who love and take better care of other people, their pets, and even their plants than they love and take care of their own bodies. Or they take good care of certain parts of their bodies (i.e., face, hair, nails) and neglect the rest. Well, if that's you, this is the time for you to start loving, knowing, accepting and taking the best care of your whole body, from head to toe, because nobody is going to do that for you. This is personal. It's all on you!

This is your time to pay attention to your one and only body and give it the love and attention it deserves and needs. Don't take your body for granted. Don't abuse it in any way or allow anyone to abuse it. I'm sure you want the best for you and the best starts in you. How you feel, value and appreciate your body will influence the decisions you make about your body.

As you know, life is all about making choices. What am I having for dinner? What should I wear to work tomorrow? Should I walk or jog later?

Same way you make decisions about your body. You decide what you do with it, what you put in it, what you allow others to do with it, and how you take care of it. Your decisions (amongst other things) will determine whether you live a long and good quality life or not. Therefore, you really want to pay attention and make the best choices that will help your body age healthfully, beautifully and gracefully.

I'll tell you right now, I love, value, and appreciate my body. It's the only one God gave me. I want a body that functions to its best and fullest potential and can take me around comfortably while I'm alive. When we go to heaven, we'll have perfect heavenly bodies (1 Corinthians 15:35-55).

While I'm still here with my uniquely imperfect body, I plan to continue treating it like God's temple and give it the best care ever, with God's help, so I can age healthfully, beautifully and gracefully in it. And hopefully live a long and good quality life, God's will. Do you want the same for yourself? I'm sure you do. We're doing this together.

> *"Know that the Lord is God. It is he who made us, and we are his; we are his people, the sheep of his pasture."*
>
> *Psalm 100:3 (NIV)*

You are Somebody to God

I think by now you know that you were magnificently made. You are not an accident! You were purposefully uniquely made by God. You have your own DNA (deoxyribonucleic acid) that is unique to you. Most important, you are somebody to God, your Heavenly Father. He knew you before you were born and He knows you by name. Awww!

God knows everything about you. Have you ever seriously thought about that? Yes, He knows everything about you, and I mean everything. He knows things you don't even know about yourself. Above all, God loves you, cares for you, and is interested in every detail of your life. You are important to Him.

At times you may feel like you are a nobody for all kinds of reasons. Or people might say things or treat you in ways to make you feel like you are nobody. But when that happens, please don't let that bad feeling last for too long. Shake it off and know that to God, you are and will always be His somebody. That's what really matters, and frankly, that's the only thing that should matter to you. I know this may be easier said than done, but try your best not to allow the things people say or do to you mess with your mind and mess you up.

When you feel like nobody, remember, you are God's precious daughter. You were fearfully and wonderfully made by your Heavenly Father. You are special to God. You matter to God. You are God's somebody!

> *"The Lord directs the steps of the godly. He delights in every detail of their lives."*
>
>

Psalm 37:23 (NLT)

> *"How precious are your thoughts about me, O God. They cannot be numbered!"*
>
>

Psalm 139:17 (NLT)

> *"And the very hairs on your head are all numbered. So don't be afraid: you are more valuable to God than a whole flock of sparrows."*
>
>

Luke 12:7 (NLT)

God Sees You

⁓◡⁓

Hello! God sees you! Yes you! His eyes are on you 24/7. You can run but you can't hide from God. He has been doing this forever. He's been watching your every move and watching over you from before you were born.

"...You are the God who sees me..."
Genesis 16:13 (NLT)

"I could ask the darkness to hide me, and the light around me to become night——but even in darkness I cannot hide from you. To you the night shines as bright as day. Darkness and light are the same to you."

Psalm 139:11-12 (NLT)

"You watched me as I was being formed in utter seclusion, as I was woven together in the dark of the womb. You saw me before I was born. Every day of my life was recorded in your book. Every moment was laid out before a single day had passed."

Psalm 139:15-16 (NLT)

God sees you at your best and worst, in your highs and lows, when you are happy and sad. He sees it all. He also sees what's going on inside your heart. You can pretend everything is okay when it's not and fool the world, but you can't fool God. He sees you and knows the truth about you. When you have secrets that nobody knows, God knows your secrets. When you think no one is watching you, guess who's eyes are on you? God's! You got that right!

> *"You know when I sit down or stand up. You know my thoughts even when I'm far away. You see me when I travel and when I rest at home. You know everything I do. You know what I'm going to say even before I say it, Lord."*
>
> *Psalm 139:2-4 (NLT)*

I truly believe that if we have awareness of God's presence, that would deter us from thinking, saying, and doing things we shouldn't be thinking, saying, or doing. We'd be mindful of our thoughts, words, actions, interactions, and reactions. But we just don't think about God in that way because we don't see Him. Out of sight, out of mind. Right? Here's the bottom line, although you don't see God, He sees you.

I didn't always have awareness of God and I know why. It was because I knew of God but didn't know Him. Therefore, I really never thought of God watching my every move. I learned that there is a big difference between knowing of God and knowing God. I was 37 years old when I rededicated my life to God and that's when I started to know Him and became aware of His presence. I'll tell you, I feel His presence every day, all day. I talk with Him about everything, every day, all day. When I'm alone, I never feel lonely because He's always with me.

> *"Don't be afraid, for I am with you. Don't be discouraged, for I am your God. I will strengthen you and help you. I will hold you up with my victorious right hand."*
>
> *Isaiah 41:10 (NLT)*

Now let's talk about your home. Even in the privacy of your home, there's no privacy with God. What goes on in your home, God sees it. Your personal business is God's business. I hope you know that.

> "Nothing in all creation is hidden from God. Everything is naked and exposed before his eyes, and he is the one to whom we are accountable."
>
> *Hebrews 4:13 (NLT)*

So, let's talk about what's going on in your home. Is everything okay in the privacy of your home? Or is there mental, emotional or physical abuse? If you are a victim of any type of abuse, please seek professional help. Is there addiction, i.e., drugs, porn, alcohol, gambling, food, sex, shopping, social media? If you have an addiction, please seek professional help. Or maybe your family is having a tough time with health, finances, kids, aging parents, or work. You may be able to hide these things from the outside world, but God sees it all. Whatever it is, call on God and He will help you. He will be with you, give you what you need and get you through whatever you're going through. God loves you! Trust God.

> "The Lord says, "I will rescue those who love me. I will protect those who trust in my name. When they call on me, I will answer; I will be with them in trouble. I will rescue and honor them. I will reward them with a long life and give them my salvation."
>
> *Psalm 91:14-16 (NLT)*

> "And may you have the power to understand, as all God's people should, how wide, how long, how high, and how deep his love is. May you experience the love of Christ, though it is too great to understand fully. Then you will be made complete with all the fullness of life and power that comes from God."
>
> *Ephesians 3:18-19 (NLT)*

When you are by yourself, how are you really doing? When you think about your life, your future, family, uncertainties, difficulties, problems, challenges and struggles you are facing, do you break down crying, fall apart or lose it? Are you hurting or grieving? Please know that God sees you and feels every bit of what you're feeling and going through. You don't want people to know your heartbreak, pain, and hurt so you hide it from them but God knows. His eyes are always on you, as a loving, caring, good and devoted Father watching over you. Nobody watches you 24/7 like God does. He is the only one who does that.

"The Lord is like a father to his children, tender and compassionate to those who fear him."

Psalm 103:13 (NLT)

"The Lord himself watches over you! The Lord stands beside you as your protective shade. The sun will not harm you by day, nor the moon at night. The Lord keeps you from all harm and watches over your life. The Lord keeps watch over you as you come and go, both now and forever."

Psalm 121:5-8 (NLT)

You are God's Masterpiece

～⦵〇～

Hey, wonderful! You are God's masterpiece. Yes, you are! You are fearfully and wonderfully made by God. In other words, you were awesomely made. There is no one else like you. Too awesome!

I know I am God's masterpiece and so are you. I know that I am fearfully and wonderfully made. And you are too. You better believe that.

I'm sure you've heard, "You are what you think you are." So, do you think you're God's masterpiece? Do you believe you are fearfully and wonderfully made? If you don't, then we're going to work on changing your mindset right now. Because when you change the way you think about yourself, then the way you feel about yourself will change. Got it? Are you ready to change your mindset? Let's do it!

Now, this is what I'd like you to do. Whenever you look in the mirror, tell yourself aloud, "I am God's masterpiece. I'm fearfully and wonderfully made." In the morning, at night or anytime you start thinking and feeling otherwise about yourself, tell yourself, "I am God's masterpiece. I'm fearfully and wonderfully made." Keep saying this to yourself, over and over again—and believe it.

You know what? Over time you will believe what you are saying to yourself and you will know that you are God's masterpiece and that you are fear-fully and wonderfully made. And every time you look in the mirror, you'll see yourself that way. You'll see yourself the way God sees you. If God said it, you better believe it. That's why you have to make the most and get the most out of God's masterpiece.

> *"I praise you because I am fearfully and wonderfully made; your works are wonderful, I know that full well."*
>
> *Psalm 139:14 (NIV)*

> *"For we are God's masterpiece. He has created us anew in Christ Jesus, so we can do the good things he planned for us long ago."*
>
> *Ephesians 2:10 (NLT)*

Speak and Claim Your Victory

Sometimes we are our own worst enemy. Instead of speaking and claiming victory, we speak and claim defeat. We know that words matter and they are powerful; therefore, we really need to pay attention to the things we say about ourselves and others.

> *"And I tell you this, you must give an account on judgment day for every idle word you speak. The words you say will either acquit you or condemn you."*
>
> *Matthew 12:36-37 (NLT)*

What you say about yourself is very important because it will most likely determine the course of your life. So, watch what you are saying about yourself. You need to say what God has said about you and be in agreement with Him. Remember, you are His precious daughter and His masterpiece. God loves you and only wants the best for you. He wants you to be the best you and live your best life here and now to be continued in heaven. And you should want the same for yourself.

"Wise words are like deep waters; wisdom flows from the wise like a bubbling brook."

Proverbs 18:4 (NLT)

"Wise words satisfy like a good meal; the right words bring satisfaction."

Proverbs 18:20 (NLT)

Unfortunately, sometimes we don't reach our full potential, achieve our dreams or we limit how far we go in life, what we achieve, and our successes because of the words we speak. When you speak negative words, words of defeat and failure, these words might just materialize themselves in your life. If you are doing this, I encourage you to change the words you are speaking right now.

"The tongue can bring death or life; those who love to talk will reap the consequences."

Proverbs 18:21 (NLT)

Every day and all through the day speak and claim God's truth about you and His promises for you. Speak and claim victory every day, all day. Yes! Speak and claim victory over all things and everything because remember, the battle is not yours, it's the Lord's (2 Chronicles 20:15). Believe in your heart that you will receive all the good things God has planned for you (Jeremiah 29:11) and that He will finish the good work He began in you (Philippians 1:6), no matter the obstacles you may face along the way. This is how you should speak, with confidence and trusting God, in Jesus' name.

Stand firm on God's Word, His promises of love, peace, joy, hope, strength, comfort, encouragement, courage, determination, perseverance, resilience, and empowerment. His Word will keep you going when the going gets tough, stay sane when you feel like you're losing your mind, and will equip you with everything you need to face life's ups and downs. God's Word will keep your faith strong even when you feel weak.

Remember, Jesus relied on God's Word all the time and used scriptures when He was tempted by the devil and the devil went away (Matthew 4:1-11). In their back and forth, the devil responded with scriptures because even the devil and his angels know scriptures, because they know the power of God's Word. And they also know how to use it against you or to confuse you, so beware. That's why you must know scriptures for yourself, have them deep rooted in your heart, that way you will not be deceived or defeated. Instead, you will be wise and victorious. God's Word is one of your most valuable weapons to defeat the devil (Ephesians 6:17).

Start right now speaking and claiming the victory God promised you!

I am blessed.

"Wherever you go and whatever you do, you will be blessed."

Deuteronomy 28:6 (NLT)

The Lord will defeat my enemies.

"The Lord will conquer your enemies when they attack you. They will attack you from one direction, but they will scatter from you in seven."

Deuteronomy 28:7 (NLT)

I am the head and not the tail. I will always be on the top and never at the bottom.

"If you listen to these commands of the Lord your God that I am giving you today, and if you carefully obey them, the Lord will make you the head and not the tail, and you will always be on top and never at the bottom."

Deuteronomy 28:13 (NLT)

The battle is not mine, it's the Lord's.

"...This is what the Lord says: Do not be afraid! Don't be discouraged by his mighty army, for the battle is not yours, but God's."

2 Chronicles 20:15 (NLT)

God fills me with His joy.

"I will be filled with joy because of you. I will sing praises to your name, O Most High."

Psalm 9:2 (NLT)

The Lord restores my soul.

"The Lord is my shepherd, I shall not be in want. He makes me lie down in green pastures, he leads me beside quiet waters, he restores my soul..."

Psalm 23:1-3 (NIV)

God is my protector.

"The Lord is my light and my salvation—so why should I be afraid? The Lord is my fortress, protecting me from danger; so why should I tremble?"

Psalm 27:1 (NLT)

God is my refuge and strength.

"God is our refuge and strength, always ready to help in times of trouble."

Psalm 46:1 (NLT)

I will rejoice every day.

"This is the day the Lord has made.We will rejoice and be glad in it."

Psalm 118:24 (NLT)

Jesus heals me.

> "But he was pierced for our transgressions, he was crushed for our iniquities; the punishment that brought us peace was upon him, and by his wounds we are healed."

Isaiah 53:5 (NIV)

God's plans for me are good.

> "For I know the plans I have for you," says the Lord. "They are plans for good and not for disaster, to give you a future and a hope."

Jeremiah 29:11 (NLT)

With God, all things are possible.

> "Jesus looked at them and said, "With man this is impossible, but with God all things are possible.""

Matthew 19:26 (NIV)

I believe that I will receive what I ask for.

> "You can pray for anything, and if you have faith, you will receive it."

Matthew 21:22 (NLT)

Nothing can separate me from the love of God.

> "For I am convinced that neither death nor life, neither angels nor demons, neither present nor future, nor any powers, neither height nor depth, nor anything else in all creation, will be able to separate us from the love of God that is in Christ Jesus our Lord."

Romans 8:38-39 (NIV)

God will give me more than I ask for or can imagine.

"Now all glory to God, who is able, through His mighty power at work within us, to accomplish infinitely more than we might ask or think."

Ephesians 3:20 (NLT)

God will finish the good work He began in me.

"And I am certain that God, who began the good work within you, will continue his work until it is finally finished on the day when Christ Jesus returns."

Philippians 1:6 (NLT)

God told me not to worry, but instead pray and give thanks, and He will give me His peace.

"Don't worry about anything; instead, pray about everything. Tell God what you need, and thank him for all he has done. Then you will experience God's peace, which exceeds anything we can understand. His peace will guard your hearts and minds as you live in Christ Jesus."

Philippians 4:6-7 (NLT)

I will think about excellent things.

"...Fix your thoughts on what is true, and honorable, and right, and pure, and lovely, and admirable. Think about things that are excellent and worthy of praise."

Philippians 4:8 (NLT)

God is my provider.

"And my God will meet all your needs according to his glorious riches in Christ Jesus."

Philippians 4:19 (NIV)

God has given me a spirit of power, love and self-discipline.

"For God has not given us a spirit of fear and timidity; but of power, love, and self-discipline."

2 Timothy 1:7 (NLT)

I walk by faith, not by sight.

"Faith is the confidence that what we hope for will actually happen; it gives us assurance about things we cannot see."

Hebrews 11:1 (NLT)

What words are you speaking into your life? Are you speaking words of victory or defeat? Remember, you can hear what you're saying about yourself. So, be mindful about what you're saying about yourself. If you're speaking defeat, failure and negativity, change it right now to victory, success and positivity.

Your victory… speak it and claim it!

You are Uniquely Beautiful

H i, beautiful! Oh yes, you are uniquely beautiful! God made each woman uniquely beautiful and that's a beautiful thing. We have different skin tones, features, we come in all heights, shapes and sizes, and have our own personalities.

Check this out… God didn't say that you are beautiful only if you have certain features or you're a certain age, color, height, weight or size. No, He didn't! Therefore, don't allow anyone to tell you or make you think or feel otherwise. Do not give anyone that kind of power over your thinking and feelings. Believe what God said… period. He said He made everything beautiful.

"He has made everything beautiful in its time…"

Ecclesiastes 3:11 (NIV)

We have our own likes and dislikes and signature styles. Different things make us feel and look beautiful, i.e., hairstyles, eyebrows, makeup, smile, the way we talk, walk, stand, mannerisms, attitudes, clothes, shoes, jewelry, accessories, handbags, perfumes, you name it. Thank God for making each woman uniquely beautiful. YAY! If we were all alike… boring.

One thing we women do need to understand, we are uniquely beautiful, and no woman is better or lesser than the other. We are physically different, and we have different personalities and passions and our own ways... to each her own. But one thing we have in common is that we're all God's daughters. God makes no distinction and shows no preference, and we shouldn't either.

Sometimes women have a tendency to compare—not a good idea. We should stay away from comparing because we all have different attributes and qualities, fortes and flaws. There are things you have that I don't have and there are things I have that you don't have. That's just the way it is and that is okay.

"And I will be your Father, and you will be my sons and daughters, says the Lord Almighty."

2 Corinthians 6:18 (NLT)

Instead of comparing, let's complement each other and help each other. Because when and where I am weak, you may be strong, and you can help me. Conversely, when and where you are weak, I may be strong and I will help you. Too, there are times when comparing leads to jealousy, envy and competition (even if only in your mind). Not good! We'll talk more about this later on.

Another thing we women tend to do is criticize each other. How she looks, what she is wearing, look at her hair, and on and on. Not nice! I'm not saying we shouldn't give advice or suggestions to each other. What I'm saying is, let's do it in a positive way, let's uplift and build up and not degrade and tear down.

"There are "friends" who destroy each other, but a real friend sticks closer than a brother."

Proverbs 18:24 (NLT)

"As iron sharpens iron, so a friend sharpens a friend."

Proverbs 27:17 (NLT)

Again, we are all different. No two women are alike. You may have things in common, but you have your differences. We like, think and do things differently. And that is not a bad thing. That is really okay.

The bottom line is, if you have good intentions and genuinely care and want to help, and what you will say is value added, then go right ahead and share your thoughts, opinions, suggestions, etc. But, as my mother would say, "If you don't have anything nice to say, don't say it."

Let's admire, compliment, complement, say nice things, be polite and kind to each other. Remember, we're all uniquely beautiful. Each one unique and precious to God. Let's love and embrace each other's unique beauty. And let's treat each other with the respect and dignity we all deserve. Celebrate your unique beauty and celebrate other women's unique beauty.

"Gentle words are a tree of life; a deceitful tongue crushes the spirit."

Proverbs 15:4 (NLT)

"Kind words are like honey—sweet to the soul and healthy for the body."

Proverbs 16:24 (NLT)

"Timely advice is lovely, like golden apples in a silver basket."

Proverbs 25:11 (NLT)

"Don't use foul or abusive language. Let everything you say be good and helpful, so that your words will be an encouragement to those who hear them."

Ephesians 4:29 (NLT)

Your Heart Matters to God

Although we are all uniquely beautiful and are different, we all have certain things in common. One of those things is our heart. God gave each one of us one heart. Your heart is important for many reasons.

We really don't think much about our heart and kind of take it for granted. That is until one day, God forbid, something goes wrong and it stops working the way it should. Then we really pay attention and maybe even panic. This is the reason why you should cherish and value every heartbeat because each one represents life. Once your heart stops beating, life is over. This is the truth of our mortality.

We all know the importance of our heart in terms of it keeping us alive, but there is so much more to it. You have an intricate, exquisite, masterful piece of heART, custom made just for you by the One and Only God Almighty (El Shaddai). How do you like your heart now?

Yes, your heart keeps you alive and that's a big deal, but there is an even bigger deal: your soul and spirit live in your heart. Did you ever think of your heart in this way? This is why your heart is so important to God. Your heart matters to God. That's the reason why He talks so profoundly about it in the Bible. Most importantly, God knows your heart. He knows what's in it.

"…The Lord doesn't see things the way you see them. People judge by outward appearance, but the Lord looks at the heart."

1 Samuel 16:7 (NLT)

Yes, what's in your heart will influence every aspect of your life and your relationships in a positive or negative way. If you're a Christian, this is critical in your relationship with God, Jesus and the Holy Spirit and your overall Christian life.

Whatever is in your heart will influence your thoughts, feelings, words, actions, how you treat yourself and others, the quality of your life and of your relationships. You want your heart to be healthy, beautiful and graceful. This is why your heart must be filled with good stuff. When your heart is filled with good stuff, there is very little room for bad stuff. And what's the good stuff? So glad you asked. Keep reading and you'll find out.

"My child, never forget the things I have taught you. Store my commands in your heart. If you do this, you will live many years, and your life will be satisfying."

Proverbs 3:1-2 (NLT)

"Let love and faithfulness never leave you; bind them around your neck, write them on the tablet of your heart. Then you will win favor and a good name in the sight of God and man."

Proverbs 3:3-4 (NIV)

"Guard your heart above all else, for it determines the course of your life."

Proverbs 4:23 (NLT)

"Wherever your treasure is, there the desires of your heart will also be."

Matthew 6:21 (NLT)

What's in Your Heart?

Many of us try all kinds of things (creams, massages, surgeries, exercise, diets, supplements, etc.) to defy nature and gravity and preserve our physical beauty longer than it would naturally last—and many women are successful. And that's all good. Because we should want to feel beautiful and look our best for a long time. But let's be honest, you can feel and look "all that" on the outside but if on the inside you're not all that, then what's inside you will detract from the outside. What do I mean by that?

You can be physically beautiful but if you have a nasty attitude, you're difficult, hard to get along with, mean, disrespectful, hateful, insensitive, selfish, etc., all of that ugliness inside you overshadows your physical beauty. Over time, people will not see your outer beauty, all they will see is that ugly side of you and will avoid you.

Inside beauty will outlast physical beauty. A beautiful heart will shine on the outside. People will see your light and feel it. They will love being around you and will want to be around you. Now, let's talk about what's in your heart. Is there beauty or ugliness? Let me just say this, we all have both, but the real question is, which one is more prevalent? Is there more beauty than ugly or the reverse?

What is a beautiful heart? A beautiful heart is genuine, loving, trustworthy, honest, warm, cheerful, kind, thoughtful, giving, positive, approachable, caring, mindful, tolerant, sensitive, encouraging, empathetic, compassionate, and treats everyone with dignity and respect no matter who they are. It's a heart filled with lots of good stuff! Let me be clear, I'm not saying that you should be perfect because none of us are or will ever be perfect (Romans 3:23). Therefore, you may not have all of these qualities, but I do hope you have many of them.

The truth is, as I said before, we all have some ugly in us. But what you want is the beauty to outshine and override the ugly. There will be times this will not happen naturally; therefore, you will have to make a conscious effort. Because there will be times that you will lose it, and that's okay. We are humans. What you don't want is for this to be the norm. You want it to be the exception, not the rule… okay.

> *"And I will give you a new heart, and I will put a new spirit in you. I will take out your stony, stubborn heart and give you a tender, responsive heart."*
>
> *Ezekiel 36:26 (NLT)*

When you have a beautiful heart, no matter who you are, how you look, what you wear or your age, you will be forever beautiful in others' eyes and you will have a lasting positive impression on anyone and everyone who crosses your path (i.e., family, friends, co-workers, classmates, neighbors, strangers). And that's a beautiful thing. Don't you think so?

If you are a Christian, the Holy Spirit will help you and guide you. But you have to ask for help and guidance, in Jesus' name. Then what the Holy Spirit will do is make sure that all that beauty outshines and overrides everything else that's in your heart. Moreover, the Holy Spirit will fill you up with the Fruit of the Spirit: love, peace, joy, patience, faith, kindness, goodness and self-control. That's what I'm talking about! I love the Holy Spirit! He's my best friend and I hope He's yours too. He keeps me in God's will.

"But the fruit of the Spirit is love, joy, peace, patience, kindness, goodness, faithfulness, gentleness and self-control. Against such things there is no law."

Galatians 5:22-23 (NIV)

If you are not a Christian, you're probably saying, "What is Deb talking about?" Let me explain. When you accept Jesus Christ as your Lord and Savior, He will live in you through the Holy Spirit. The Holy Spirit will help and guide you through your life and in every area of your life, and will change you to be more like Jesus. The Holy Spirit will fill you up with all God's good stuff. That's some good stuff right there.

"But whenever someone turns to the Lord, the veil is taken away. For the Lord is the Spirit, and wherever the Spirit of the Lord is; there is freedom. So all of us who have had that veil removed can see and reflect the glory of the Lord. And the Lord—who is the Spirit—makes us more and more like him as we are changed into his glorious image."

2 Corinthians 3:16-18 (NLT)

Are There Negative Feelings Hidden in Your Heart?

Please take a minute to think about this… Are there negative feelings hidden in your heart? Envy, resentment, hate, grudges, unforgiveness or other negative feelings. If yes, well this is the time to let go of those feelings and let God set you free. But first you have to acknowledge that you have these negative feelings. Remember that what's in your heart influences your thoughts, feelings, words, actions, how you treat yourself and others, the quality of your life and of your relationships. In a nutshell, the way you live your life.

I know for a fact that there are times we don't know we have negative feelings hidden in our hearts. Not until someone tells us or God reveals it to us. Well, that's exactly what happened to me. In 1999 when I rededicated my life to God and surrendered ALL to Him, God revealed to me that I had resentment in my heart. He told me that I had to let go so I could receive the fullness of His blessing.

This caught me totally by surprise, because I didn't know I had any resentment. Then God brought names to my mind and I felt a tingling in my heart each time and that's how I knew, oh yes, I had resentment. I'll be honest, I cried. But God, being a loving, caring and merciful Father, told me exactly what I needed to do to let it go. He told me to write a letter to each person and let them know how I felt and why, and that's exactly what I did. It was hard and brought back memories and feelings I really didn't want to deal with. But after I was done, God set me free. What an awesome feeling.

And you know what? God kept His promise to me. He sure did. He has blessed me in ways I never imagined and given me more than I ever asked for and continues to do so every day. And He has used ordinary me in many special ways for His honor and glory and to bless many. I'm so thankful to God for His unconditional love, steadfast faithfulness and for not giving up on me. God knew my heart and He knew that one day it will belong to Him. I love Him so much!

Today I can say that the beauty in me outshines and overrides the ugly and brings out the best me and makes me do the right thing even when I don't feel like doing the right thing. God always tells me, "Debbie, you do the right thing and leave the rest to Me." The best part is that God is using me to speak to your heart right now. He wants the beauty in you to rise and shine and bring out the best you, so you can live your best life here and now to be continued in heaven. Oh, I'm so happy for you!

I encourage you to take this time to examine your heart. Take a moment to self-reflect. Ask yourself, what's in my heart? Is my heart beautiful or ugly? Are there any negative feelings hidden in my heart? List all of the good and bad stuff in your heart. Does the good outweigh the bad? Ask God to remove the bad stuff and negative feelings and fill your heart with good stuff and positive feelings. Are you ready to let go of any negative feeling? Ask God to set you free! Let your beautiful heart rise and shine.

"Trust in the Lord and do good. Then you will live safely in the land and prosper. Take delight in the Lord, and he will give you your heart's desires."

Psalm 37:3-4 (NLT)

"Create in me a clean heart, O God. Renew a loyal spirit within me."

Psalm 51:10 (NLT)

"Search me, O God, and know my heart; test me and know my anxious thoughts. See if there is any offensive way in me, and lead me in the way everlasting."

Psalm 139:23-24 (NIV)

Give Your Heart to Jesus!

M y dear Sister in Christ, I can't let this moment go by without extending an invitation to give your heart to Jesus Christ and accept Him as your Lord and Savior, if you haven't already. Jesus died and rose on the third day so you and I can live forever with God and Him in heaven. This is the biggest decision you'll ever make in your lifetime. It is literally a life or death decision. There is no better time than now to just do it! Please know that Jesus is the only way to God and the only way to heaven. Seal your final destination now and start your wonderful life changing journey today.

> "For then the dust will return to the earth, and the spirit will return to God who gave it."
>
> *Ecclesiastes 12:7 (NLT)*

> "Then Jesus said, "Come to me, all of you who are weary and carry heavy burdens, and I will give you rest."
>
> *Matthew 11:28 (NLT)*

> "For God loved the world so much that he gave his one and only Son, so

that everyone who believes in him will not perish but have eternal life. God sent his Son into the world not to judge the world, but to save the world through him."

John 3:16-17 (NLT)

"Jesus answered, "I am the way and the truth and the life. No one comes to the Father except through me."

John 14:6 (NIV)

I was 37 years old when my wonderful life changing journey with God began. For 21 years God has been working for me, in me, and through me. My relationship with God gets stronger and stronger every day. And I've been steadily growing in faith and in His Word. However, I'm still a work in progress and I'm loving it.

I'm definitely not the same girl I was 21 years ago. I'm wiser, better, blessed and highly favored. And I don't say this because it sounds good. I say this because this is my truth. And I'm not talking about material stuff, I'm talking about Spiritual stuff that last forever. Say yes to Jesus and start your wonderful life changing journey with God right now.

"All praise to God, the Father of our Lord Jesus Christ, who has blessed us with every spiritual blessing in the heavenly realms because we are united with Christ."

Ephesians 1:3 (NLT)

When you give your heart to Jesus, you will become a member of God's Family along with many of us, your brothers and sisters. As I mentioned before, once you accept Jesus, the Holy Spirit will be in you and with you, guiding you through life's ups and downs, keeping you in God's will. God and Jesus will always be with you through the Holy Spirit. You may not understand all this right now, but you will in time, as you get closer and closer to God and

Jesus, and get to know Them personally.

You will no longer have to face life's challenges on your own, by yourself, because as God promised, He will be with you always, giving you love, comfort, joy, peace and hope, and getting you through each one, victoriously. I'm telling you what I know firsthand. I've experienced God to His fullest. He has been with me in my darkest times and only because of Him I've gotten through each one. He is my rock during difficult times. His love, mercy and faithfulness are immeasurable.

There are no words that can aptly explain my God experience. But one thing I can tell you, God and I have the best Father-daughter relationship ever. And the best part is that you can too. You can have the same awesome relationship, because God is not exclusive, He is inclusive. He is here for anyone who accepts His Son Jesus, no matter what you look like, the color of your skin, social status, political affiliation, rich or poor, etc. Because God knows your heart and that's what matters to Him.

"For whoever finds me finds life and receives favor from the Lord."

Proverbs 8:35 (NLT)

"But to all who believed him and accepted him, he gave the right to become children of God. They are reborn—not with a physical birth resulting from human passion or plan, but a birth that comes from God."

John 1:12-13 (NLT)

"See how very much our Father loves us, for he calls us his children, and that is what we are! But the people who belong to this world don't recognize that we are God's children because they don't know him."

1 John 3:1 (NLT)

Start your own God experience today. Say the Prayer of Salvation. Confess your sins to God and ask Him to forgive you. Turn your life and your future over to God through Jesus and be led by the Holy Spirit. Watch God change you without you realizing it. It is amazing. And guess what? You will be the best you and live your best life here and now to be continued in heaven.

Prayer of Salvation

Let's pray…

Heavenly Father, I come to You in the Name of Jesus.

I am calling on You according to Acts 2:21 (NIV): "And everyone who calls on the name of the Lord will be saved."

I confess my sins and ask for Your forgiveness.

I pray and ask Jesus to come into my heart and be Lord over my life according to Romans 10:9-10 (NLT): *"If you confess with your mouth that Jesus is Lord and believe in your heart that God raised him from the dead, you will be saved. For it is by believing in your heart that you are made right with God, and it is by confessing with your mouth that you are saved."* I do that now.

I confess that Jesus is Lord, and I believe in my heart that God raised Him from the dead. Amen

> *"…But as for me and my family, we will serve the Lord."*
>
> *Joshua 24:15 (NLT)*

I encourage you to join a Bible preaching and teaching church and a Bible study group to connect with other believers to fellowship, pray, praise, worship, grow and strengthen your faith and learn God's Word. Also, on your own, pray and read your Bible, this will enrich and bless your life in ways you can't imagine. All these things combined will help you develop a close and personal relationship with God and Jesus. And your soul and spirit will be healthy, beautiful and graceful. Alleluia!

Surrender ALL to God

After accepting Jesus Christ as your Lord and Savior, there is one more life changing decision to make: Surrender ALL to God! This will take your relationship with God to the next level. I know this personally. This will certainly position you to be the best you and live your best life here and now to be continued in heaven.

Unfortunately, there are Christians, new and old, who have not done this yet or think they have but really haven't. If you're feeling that something is missing in your Christian life, it may well be that you've not surrendered ALL to God. Have you surrendered your will, life and future to God? Please take a moment to think this through.

What does surrendering ALL to God mean? It means turning over everything, and I mean everything, to God and trusting Him. The truth is, many of us are just not ready to do that so we keep holding on to stuff. We want to lean on our own understanding and on our own strength. We want to handle things on our own and do things our way instead of turning things over to God, leaning on Him and doing things His way.

Sometimes we mistakenly think that surrendering ALL to God is a sign of weakness, when in reality it's a sign of strength because when we're weak, God makes us strong for His honor and glory. God, through Jesus, empowers you to accomplish things you can't even imagine and equips you with whatever you need to overcome and get through any situation. I encourage you to surrender ALL to God right now and experience God to His fullest.

> *"That is why, for Christ's sake, I delight in weaknesses, in insults, in hardships, in persecutions, in difficulties. For when I am weak, then I am strong."*
>
> *2 Corinthians 12:10 (NIV)*

Prayer is Powerful

Prayer is the most effective way to communicate and connect with God. Pray, pray, pray and don't stop praying, especially during difficult times because there is mighty power in prayer. Through prayer, Jesus makes things happen.

When facing difficult times, you want to take your prayer to the next level. Here are the prayer steps that works for me, every time, and I know will work for you. I encourage you to read the scriptures I'm referencing and meditate.

1. Write down your prayer and date it. Writing down your prayer is important and takes your prayer to another level (Habakkuk 2:2). This means you're serious, you're not playing, you're desperate, you really need a change, you need a breakthrough, you want things to turn around in a good way. You need God!

2. Be specific about what you are asking God for with a sincere and clean heart. Being specific makes you think through what you are asking for. Sometimes when we have to write things down, we get stuck and don't know what to write because we really don't know what we want or why we want it, and this puts things into perspective. You want to be as detailed as possible because when you receive what you asked for, you know without a doubt that it came from God (James 1:17).

3. Reference scriptures that relate to your situation throughout your prayer (Hebrews 4:12). This is not for God's benefit but for your benefit. It reassures you that if God said it or did it for someone else, He will do the same for you. Also remember that when Jesus was tempted by the devil, His response was, "It is written." Jesus defeated the devil and resisted temptation three times by quoting scriptures (Matthew 4:1-11). If Jesus, the Son of God, relied on scripture, how much more should we. Hello!

4. Thank God for what He has done, is doing, and will do for you. God loves you, cares for you and is interested in every detail of your life. He is always doing good things for you, small and big. God is always working behind the scenes for you, lining up things and positioning things for your good. He is that awesome! Many times, we credit the good things in our lives to "good luck" when in reality, it's "God's love" that's working miracles in our lives (Psalm 136:1-4).

5. Pray in Jesus' name. Why? Because that's what Jesus said to do. Got it! We

must pray to God in Jesus' name because Jesus is the only way to God (John 14:6; 16:23-24). There is no name greater than the name of Jesus. His name is above all names (Philippians 2:9). When you call on the name of Jesus believing that you will receive what you asked for, make no mistake, God will deliver, and you might even get more than what you asked for (Ephesians 3:20).

6. Agreement Verses. Write a list of scriptures about God's promises that relate to your situation that comfort, encourage and uplift you. Read them aloud and allow scripture, through the Holy Spirit, to speak to your heart and to your situation. Take a moment to meditate on each scripture. Reflect on what it means to you. Make scripture personal... own it. Make it your reality and apply it in your life. Trust God to do what He promised. Because "God is not a man, so he does not lie" Numbers 23:19 (NLT).

7. Pray in Agreement. Share your written prayer and agreement verses with people you trust and agree in prayer. Prayer is already powerful, but when two or three are praying the exact same thing and agree, this is extra powerful (Matthew 18:19-20).

8. Pray daily without ceasing. Spend quiet time with God. Don't rush through this. You may want to first start with praising and worshipping God with Christian music to focus your mind and heart on God. Then aloud, read your agreement verses, meditate on them, pray your agreement prayer, then talk with God straight from your heart, in Jesus' name. Pray without ceasing (1 Thessalonians 5:16). You will feel God's presence, love, peace and joy. You will start to see God working all things together for your good (Romans 8:28), even bad things.

"I love the Lord because he hears my voice and my prayer for mercy. Because he bends down to listen, I will pray as long as I have breath!"

Psalm 116:1-2 (NLT)

"Again, I tell you that if two of you on earth agree about anything you ask for, it will be done for you by my Father in heaven. For where two or three come together in my name, I am with them."

Matthew 18:19-20 (NIV)

"Devote yourselves to prayer, being watchful and thankful."

Colossians 4:2 (NIV)

"...Yet you don't have what you want because you don't ask God for it. And even when you ask, you don't get it because your motives are all wrong—you want only what will give you pleasure."

James 4:2-3 (NLT)

"Confess your sins to each other and pray for each other so that you may be healed. The earnest prayer of a righteous person has great power and produces wonderful results."

James 5:16 (NLT)

Read and Study Your Bible

I encourage you to read and study your Bible. This is one way to get to know God, Jesus and the Holy Spirit and to develop a close and personal relationship with Them. You'll learn about God's plan and promises for your life and how to live a Christian life. Then you will live a spirit-filled, spirit-led and spirit-thrilled Christian life.

This is another way to spend quiet time with God. This is the time God talks to your heart and connects with your Spirit through His Word. This is when God, through Jesus,

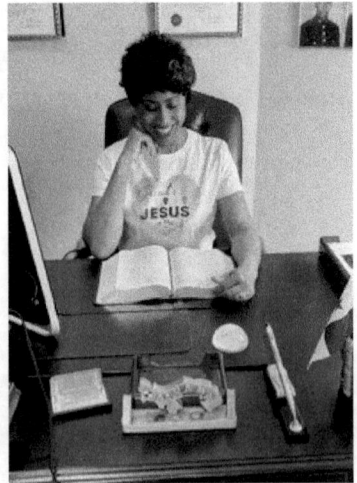

strengthens you, reassures you, and grows your faith. This is your time to hang out with God, learn and get filled with His Word. You want God's Word to be deep rooted in your heart, so you can use it when you need it to get you through whatever life throws at you, just like it did for Jesus.

The Bible is your life manual, your lifeline. It sure is. Everything you need to know about life and what to do when faced with adversities is in the Bible. It's all in there.

Also, when you know God's Word, you will know His truth and you will be able to discern what's from God and what's not from God. Because not every person who says they represent Jesus are truly representing Jesus (Matthew 24:24-27).

Before you start reading your Bible, ask God to give you clear understanding and to reveal His truth to you. Ask for His Word to speak directly to your heart and to your situation, and then incorporate these teachings into your daily living.

Reading the Bible may be challenging at first and maybe even boring. I know it was for me. That's why I never got pass Genesis. However, I did know Bible stories because my mom had read them to me, then as I got older I loved reading them and I learned them in Sunday School and watching television.

To be totally honest, I didn't read the Bible from cover to cover until August 23, 2003 when I was 41 years old, after I rededicated my life to God in fall 1999. I remember one day in 2001 while I was in quiet time with God, He asked me, "What are you going to answer Me when I ask you why didn't you read My Bible from cover to cover? You read everything else." I was in shock to say the least and immediately went into panic.

I started reading the Bible every day and asked God to please not let me die before reading it in its entirety, because I didn't want to have to answer that question. Thank God I finally read the Bible from cover to cover and have read it a few more times. Talk about feeling pressure. Whew! Let me tell you, reading the Bible made a huge difference in my life and I guarantee it will do the same for you.

The awesome news is that there are many Bible translations now and that's a beautiful thing. I was so happy when I found two translations that were easy to read, follow, and understand. I encourage you, if you haven't already, to find a translation that's easy for you to read and understand. Some people have said that one of the reasons they don't read the Bible is because it's too hard to understand, mainly talking about the King James Version (KJV). I felt the same way. But now with so many Bible translations to choose from, that reason no longer holds water. Here are a few translations to consider: New International Version (NIV), New King James Version (NKJV), New American Standard Bible (NASB), New Living Translation (NLT) and English Standard Version (ESV).

Another reason why some say they don't read the Bible is because it's boring. I felt the same way, especially when I got to the scriptures in Genesis that talked about the descendants; this is where it all went downhill. I made several attempts to read the Bible and every time I got to that spot, I just could not get past it and would end up stopping. In 2001 when I felt the pressure to read the Bible, I asked God for guidance. The Holy Spirit told me to start reading the New Testament first and that made the difference for me.

When people say to me that they want to read the Bible but sound unsure how to go about it, I always suggest to start reading the New Testament first, from Matthew through Jude. Let me give you a synopsis.

The first four books in the New Testament, known as the gospels, are four individual accounts of Jesus' life, ministry, and death. Followed by Acts, the fifth book, where the twelve apostles start spreading the gospel of salvation as Jesus told them to do (Matthew 28:18-20). The other books through Jude cover Christian living principles that were applicable in those days and are still relevant and applicable today.

When you get to the book of Revelation—don't read it—go to the Old Testament first. When you're done reading the Old Testament, then read the book of Revelation. That's my two-cents.

I'd also like to suggest a few Bible readings to read at your leisure: Genesis

1, 2 and 3; Psalms 8, 91, 100, 139, and 150; the Ten Commandments (Exodus 20:3-17); the Beatitudes (Matthew 5:3-10); the Lord's Prayer (Matthew 6:9-13); The Lord's Supper (I Corinthians 11:23-34); The Fruit of the Spirit (Galatians 5:22-23); and the Armor of God (Ephesians 6:13-17).

"Study this Book of Instruction continually. Meditate on it day and night so you will be sure to obey everything written in it. Only then you will prosper and succeed in all you do."

Joshua 1:8 (NLT)

"All Scripture is inspired by God and is useful to teach us what is true and to make us realize what is wrong in our lives. It corrects us when we are wrong and teaches us do what is right. God uses it to prepare and equip his people to do every good work."

2 Timothy 3:16-17 (NLT)

"For the word of God is alive and powerful. It is sharper than the sharpest two-edged sword, cutting between soul and spirit, between joint and marrow. It exposes our innermost thoughts and desires."

Hebrews 4:12 (NLT)

"Blessed is the one who reads the words of this prophecy, and blessed are those who hear it and take to heart what is written in it, because the time is near."

Revelation 1:3 (NIV)

YOU!

Focus on "Your Beauty"

C elebrities have access to "the best" money can buy to make them always look beautiful, fabulous, and flawless all the time. And they should. They pay lots of money to look that way. They have a team of experts at their beck and call, working around the clock to make them look beautiful all the time.

Honestly, these women have no excuse not to look beautiful, fabulous, and flawless all the time, because they have everything money can buy at their disposal. And let's not talk about Photoshop that makes them look physically perfect. Without all that, how would they look? But you know what, I'm not mad at them. If I had that kind of money, trust me, I'd do the same.

But the truth is, I don't have that kind of money and most likely neither do you. Their reality is not my reality nor yours. That's why we have to live in our reality and within our means. The truth is, I can't do what they do, and most likely, neither can you. This is why it's important to focus on "your beauty" and buy products and do things that are affordable, within your budget, and not break the bank.

Everyday women like you and me (whether married, divorced, or single, with dependents or not) depend on a weekly, bi-weekly or monthly paycheck to pay the bills. And as you know, every woman's financial situation, money

49

management, and spending habits are different, and may change at any given time. Every woman's disposable income varies depending on what's going on in her life. Some women may not have disposable income and are living paycheck to paycheck or on a tight budget. I have been in all of these situations at different times in my life.

No matter your financial situation, you should not compare yourself to other women or focus on other women's "beauty." Don't go out of your way to do what they do or to look the way they look and find yourself in a financial bind. It is so not worth it. Instead, focus on "your beauty" and do things within your means that will make you look and feel beautiful. My mom would always say, "Live within your means." Don't get me wrong, admire and learn from other women but don't get caught-up and lose focus of you. Here's the bottom line, "be beautiful you!"

I always try to look, feel, and live my best. I like doing my own things that make me look and feel beautiful, i.e., facials, exercising, eating in moderation, wearing clothes that fit my body shape, etc. Of course, there are some things I do if and when I can afford it. To be honest, I just love being me! I don't want to look and be anyone else but me. I try to make the most and get the most out of what God has given me and make it work for me.

When you try to look like someone else, you'll never feel happy or satisfied with you because no matter how much you try, you'll never look exactly like that person because you are not her. You are you! If you see something you like on another woman and you want to try it, if you can afford it, absolutely try it. See if it looks good on you, if it is brings out your beauty.

What you want is to be beautiful you. Whatever is "your beauty," is your beauty. Just be you, do you, and feel beautiful in your own skin. Be happy with you. Feel comfortable, empowered and confident in your own beauty.

Please Do Not Compare Your Life to Others... Not Good!

I want to talk more about comparing in terms of comparing your life to others, because it can be so destructive. Comparing your life in any way, shape or form to family, friends or celebrities is not good. It is never a good idea and leads to nothing good. As I mentioned before, there are times comparing leads to jealousy, envy, and competition (even if it's only in your mind), stirring up all kinds of negative feelings and emotions towards yourself and others. Not good. Hopefully, you are not doing this but if you are, I pray this will give you a different perspective. If you are not, you might know someone that is and will share this with the person.

Unfortunately, social media provides opportunities for comparisons amongst family and friends, because for some reason people feel the need to share and sometimes over share all that's going on in their lives, whether it is real or embellished. Giving the impression, intentionally or unintentionally, that they are "living their best life" and making you feel that you are not. And the people reading these posts get caught-up, wishing they were those people and start comparing lives.

So, here we go… The readers start to feel that they're missing out on life, that their life is awful, that they are imperfect and fall short, which we all are (and this is God's truth, literally) and they are living imperfect lives, which we all are (another one of God's truth). They feel miserable, discontent and unhappy with their lives and may even fall into isolation, depression, and some even put unnecessary stress on themselves trying to keep up with the Joneses. All of this plethora of emotions sometimes leads to envy, jealousy, and competition. And I've seen it bring out the worst in people.

Also, there are people who get caught-up in celebrities' posts and compare their lives to the lives of celebrities. Nowadays, for better or worse, there is just too much information that is accessible in real time about what's going on in these people's lives. Because it financially benefits celebrities to put their stuff out there. It's business! They have to be in your face, in your ears, all day, and most important, in your pocket. That's the way they stay relevant and make money. I'm not mad at them. They've got to do what they've got to do! That's their reality.

But here's your reality, they don't know you, and you don't know them, and most likely you all will never meet. So why are you stressing, getting bent out of shape and going out of your way to keep up with somebody you don't know and most likely will never do a thing for you? While living paycheck to paycheck, trying to figure out how to make ends meet and how to pay your bills. Just keeping it real.

Here's another truth, it does not matter who you are or think you are, no one's life is perfect. Everybody has something bad or challenging going on in their life, whether it's personally or with a loved one, or professionally. So when you're reading other people's posts, take it with a grain of salt and keep things in perspective.

This is why you should not compare your life to others. You really don't know what's going on in their lives and behind closed doors. Because no one tells everything on social media. Everybody gives snippets of whatever they want the world to know or think about them. Also, not everything posted on social media is true and real.

Here's the deal: More times than not, when you go down the road of comparing, you will get lost. There will be hurt feelings, you may feel lesser than others, unappreciated, not loved as much as the other person. Your self-esteem and self-confidence may be compromised, families stop talking to each other, friendships break-up and things quickly spiral out of control. I've seen all of these things happen. Nothing good comes out of comparing. It is not healthy and there is no value added.

Let's say that good things are happening in someone's life and the person decides to share the good news with family and friends on social media. Instead of comparing, be happy for that person. You have had your good moments and will have more good moments too. Because life is a mixed baggage of good and bad. So, hopefully when good things happen in your life and if you decide to share the good news with family and friends, they will be happy for you. You certainly would not like them to be comparing and feeling envious, jealous, or competing with you.

Don't get me wrong, I think social media is a good thing. But like everything in life, good things can be used for good and bad, and we've seen that play out many ways. It depends whose hands it's in and the motive. You just have to weigh things out. You have to be wise and keep a balance between what you put into it and take out of it, and how you process the information and use it. And ask yourself: Is it beneficial to me or is it detrimental to me? Is it building me up or tearing me down? Is it really worth my time or am I wasting my time? Just a few things to think about.

Here's the bottom line, their life is not yours. You need to stay focused on your life and what's happening in your life. If you look closely into your life, you will see good things happening too. But when you are too busy in other people's lives, you don't have time to see and appreciate all the good things going on in your life. And sometimes we take for granted the good people and good things in our lives and don't see them as such.

When you focus on the good people and the good things God has blessed you with through your life, you will realize that you are living your best life and you will not be consumed with someone else's best life. So, don't compare. Be you and do you and live your best life.

Self

As I mentioned earlier, from a young age I was always interested in taking care of my body. In those early years I was not thinking about taking care of my soul and spirit too. But today I know that taking care of my soul and spirit and keeping them healthy, beautiful, and graceful are as important as taking care of my body.

I've always loved and accepted my body with all of its imperfections. I wanted to feel good and beautiful in it. I wanted to know it and give it the best care. I've always been good with being imperfectly beautiful. But I know women who struggle with body image; they don't love and accept their body, and are always finding faults. And there are women who don't know their body and don't take care of it. Let's talk about this.

You love, accept, know and care for loved ones with all of their imperfections. Right? There are things you may not like about them and wish they would change, but you still love and accept them anyway. So why not give yourself a break and treat yourself the same way you treat your loved ones? If you haven't been doing that, this is the perfect time to start. Okay.

Think about this: The body you are in is the only body you'll forever have.

So why not love it, accept it, know it and take the best care of it with all of its imperfections? Why not make it feel and look its best? I encourage you and challenge you to make the most and get the most out of your body. And age healthfully, beautifully and gracefully in it. Are you ready to take the challenge? Yes you are!

Let's get right to it…

Self Love

We all know that love is the most powerful emotion in humans. When Jesus said, "Love your neighbor as yourself," that tells me that God expects us to love ourselves (God first of course). It also tells me that you have to love yourself so you know how to love others. Did you ever think of this?

> *"Teacher, which is the greatest commandment in the Law?" Jesus replied, "'Love the Lord your God with all your heart and with all your soul and with all your mind. This is the first and greatest commandment. And the second is like it: 'Love your neighbor as yourself.' All the Law and the Prophets hang on these two commandments."*

> *Matthew 22:36-40 (NIV)*

Loving others and feeling loved are two of the best feelings you can experience. Hands down, love will bring out the best in you and the best in others. Also, love will make you want the best for yourself and the best for others. When there is love, everybody wins. All of this loving is super important in our lives and self-love is as important. Do you believe this?

When you love yourself, you are thanking God for His most valuable work of art—you. You are acknowledging that your body is God's temple, that you were fearfully and wonderfully made. That you are God's masterpiece! You will accept you in every way, with all of your imperfections. You will want to know everything about you—body, soul, and spirit—and take the best care of yourself in every respect.

You will love spending time with you, and look forward to spending time with yourself. You will enjoy hanging out with you and not feel like a fish out of water when you are by yourself and not surrounded by people. You will know your worth and won't be dependent on others' validation or acceptance to feel worthy.

In addition to all the above, self-love will empower and build your self-confidence and self-esteem. Consequently, you will feel good about yourself, happier and comfortable in your own body. So, show yourself some love. If you haven't been doing that, I encourage you to start right now.

Self Accept

My personal belief is that we should accept ourselves from the get-go just because we know that God made us. Yes, we are imperfectly uniquely beautiful, and that's God's truth. None of us has everything we would love to have, mentally, emotionally, and physically. But you know what? If we did have everything and we were perfect, then we would not need God, Jesus and the Holy Spirit. We would be self-sufficient in every area and in every respect and would not need Them. Thank God that's not the case. That we are not perfect and we need God, Jesus, and the Holy Spirit in our lives to help us through our imperfections—mental, emotional and physical.

> *"Trust in the Lord with all your heart; do not depend on your own understanding. Seek his will in all you do, and he will show you which path to take."*
>
> *Proverbs 3:5-6 (NLT)*

You may have things you don't like about yourself or wish you could change. And guess what? You're not alone. Many women feel the same way, especially about their body. But you know what? Still accept you anyway. Sometimes we are our worst critic and don't give ourselves a break.

We need to love and show compassion towards ourselves. Life is just too short, so make the most and get the most out of you. I know what you're thinking, "Yeah right! Easier said than done. I'm not good at this or that. I struggle with this or that. My this or that is too big or too small. My hair is too this or that."

Hey, lady, I hear you. But work with what you've got. And in terms of your body, remember, this is your one and only body that has been with you your whole life and is going to be with you for the rest of your life. It is not going anywhere! No body is perfect, not one. Even those bodies that look perfect, are not perfect. Okay! We'll have perfect bodies when we go to heaven, but in the meantime, love, accept, know, and take the best care of your imperfect body. Accept your imperfections because that's what makes you, you.

When you accept your body, you're saying, "Yes, I love me just the way I am!" Is there room for improvement? Ahhh yes! Of course you want to look beautiful and your best. And the good news is, you certainly can. You can do so many things to achieve the look you want. There are many options available to help you do exactly what you want, in a safe and affordable manner.

If there are things you'd like to improve or change to make you look and feel your best, go for it. And if you are happy and good with you, just the way you are, that is awesome. Here's the bottom line: just be you and do you! But remember, for you to be you and do you, you should know who you are.

Self Know

One of the most important things that will make any relationship meaningful and strong, is knowing each other. When you love someone, you are interested and eager to know everything about that person. This takes time and effort. Taking and making time to know that special person in your life, shows you care. I'm sure you will make the time to make it happen. The truth is, sometimes we know others better than we know ourselves.

Likewise, you should be eager and interested to know everything about you—body, soul, and spirit. You should want to make time to spend quality time with you. This is so important because this helps build character, keep balance, set personal standards, set healthy boundaries, and know how to properly take care of yourself. Unfortunately, this is not the case for many. For some reason, many women don't want to get to know themselves. Some are too afraid to discover things that might make them uncomfortable or things they've been ignoring or denying.

Of course, you are a mixed baggage of good and bad. We all are. But let the good rise and shine and work on improving, managing, or getting rid of the bad. Get to know your gifts and abilities so you can use and develop them and reach your full potential. Here's the thing, what you don't know, you can't use or develop. This is a reason why many never reach their full potential or even get close and many sell themselves short.

If you don't know yourself, this is the perfect time to start. Dig deep in you to find out everything about you. Know your fortes and flaws. Get to know your fears, limitations, triggers, pet peeves, breaking points, passions, qualities, strengths, weaknesses, what you like or don't like, who or what makes you cry or smile or brings out the best or worst in you, what would you tolerate or not, etc.

If you do know yourself, this is also a good time to check in with yourself and find out if something changed. Because sometimes circumstances in our lives change us for better or worse, and we need to know and address them appropriately.

One good thing about knowing yourself (the good, bad and ugly), is that when anybody tells you about you, you will know if they are right or wrong. You will not waver or wonder because you know you. But you have to be true to yourself, acknowledge the truth about who you are, take responsibility if they are right, and take any appropriate action. But if what was said is wrong, then either address it right there and then or ignore or dismiss, either way, keep it moving and don't dwell on it. Depending on the situation, sometimes is best to ignore or dismiss. It may not be worth the effort, energy, and time.

The bottom line is when you know who you are, nobody can tell you who you are not. I had an incident once and I addressed it right there and then.

I stopped the person in their track because one thing I'm not going to have anyone do is disrespect me by telling me things about me that are not true and stay quiet. That ain't happening!

What you should be mindful about is not allowing what people say about you to have a negative effect on you mentally. You really want to rise to the occasion. Yes, we all have character flaws that can be improved or managed better. I say managed better because there are somethings we can't get rid of, we can only manage. But you have to want to do something about it. Then commit to finding ways to do better or manage better. You may even need professional help. The truth is, whatever we really want to do, we will find a way to get it done. As my mother would say, "Where there is a will, there is a way." Though, I certainly understand that asking for help is not easy at times for many reasons. But please don't feel afraid or embarrassed to ask for help. At some point in our lives we all need help.

You also want to know everything about your body, from head to toe. When you know your body, you know what's your normal because every-body's normal is different. You will know when there is a change or something just does not look or feel right. You will pay close attention to your body, monitor it, and promptly take care of anything that is not your normal.

Knowing your mental and emotional state is extremely important too. When our mind is right, we function our best. When our mind is not right, we struggle with the simplest things. We all have a breaking point, and we all have our moments. When things get to us, get out of control and become overwhelming to the point that it starts to affect us mentally and emotionally, and might even manifest itself physically, these are signs that we need to seek help. Talk to somebody you trust.

We have to know when we are reaching our breaking point and seek help as early as possible. I know people who know they need help but they don't get help because they feel they will be judged. Also, there is mental health stigma that causes people to feel ashamed and prevents them from seeking the help they need. Though the stigma has been reduced over the years, we still have a ways to go. But what we want to try to avoid as much as possible is waiting until we have reached our breaking point. Help will be there either way but like everything else, it's best to take care of yourself earlier than later.

The bottom line is, get to know you and be the best version of you.

Self Care

When you pay close attention to your body and take the best care of it, you will reap the benefits and it will positively affect the quality of your life. Keeping up with periodic dental and health examinations, drinking water, eating balanced meals and in moderation, exercising regularly, getting a good night's sleep, and other healthy habits will help maintain good health and prevent diseases for as long as possible, and will help you age healthfully, beautifully and gracefully. Isn't that what we all want? I do and I know you do too.

Next time you look in the mirror and see those things you don't like or wish you could change, stop and think of all the things you and your body have been through. Your body is the only one with you 24/7, taking you everywhere and wherever you want or need to go. It's been faithful to you so be faithful to it. Love your body and take the best care of it.

Just like a car, your body will go through wear and tear. That's why it needs routine maintenance for prevention and early detection to address any issues to keep it running in the best condition for a long time. Show your body that you love it and you care for it by taking the best care of it! Then you'll surely get the most out of it for a long time.

As I mentioned before, you also want to take care good care of your mind. You want to keep a pulse on your mental and emotional state. Pay attention to what's going on in your head, how you feel, and how it's affecting you. If you are not feeling well, because you know when you are not, please get help. Maintaining a healthy mind is an important part of living a healthy, good quality, productive, purposeful, and enjoyable long life.

We're All Dealing with Something or Somethings

彡⊙⊜彡

No matter our age, we're all dealing with something or somethings, i.e., mental, emotional, physical, or a combination. At 58 years young, I'm surely dealing with my share of stuff. God knows! If it's not one thing, it's another. Every day there's a new challenge. So, I deal with it the best way I can, with God's help, of course, and keep it moving. I try to make the most and get the most out of my life.

As I said before, sharing is caring! So, I'm going to share a few of my life challenges with you. You may be going through similar challenges or may have already. If you haven't gone through anything yet, you will, sooner or later. As we age, we all go through natural body changes and phases.

Okay, so I'm forgetful, have aches and pains, and my energy level is declining. I suffer with migraines, dizziness, and vertigo. I've had poor vision and worn glasses from the time I was about five years old. My lenses kept getting thicker and thicker with each prescription. In school I was teased a lot about my thick lenses so I was self-conscious and couldn't wait to one day wear contact lenses. I started wearing contacts when I was 19 years old. I finally got to see my face in the mirror without glasses. Wow! That was an exciting and memorable day for me

In 1999 at age 37 after I had moved to the U.S. with my family, I had to stop wearing contact lenses because my eyes were not tolerating them anymore. That meant I had to go back to wearing thicker lenses. The difference this time was that I didn't care two biscuits (as my West Indian folks would say) what people would think or say about my thick lenses. As you get older, certain things just don't matter. No one made any comments, at least not to me, and if they had, I would have ignored it and kept it moving. Don't have time to entertain negativity.

As I grew in my faith, I learned to appreciate the things that really matter. And what mattered was that I could see. God provided a way for me to see, my thick lenses. I was so grateful to God that I could see, I didn't care about anything else. So, I went right on about my business, with self-confidence, feeling and looking beautiful with my thick lenses. Okay!

July 2018 I had cataract surgeries because my eyes had gotten so bad that I was struggling to see. I had put off this surgery for as long as I could because I was afraid. This is supposed to be a common procedure with a high success rate and no complications. Unfortunately, that was not the case for my mom. So, I was nervous about the surgery because at least I could see a little. I was concerned about things going bad and not seeing at all. But God talked to me and calmed me. He told me not to worry, that He was going to be right there watching over me, making sure everything was done correctly. I felt an instant peace and I knew that everything was going to be alright. Well, as God promised, both surgeries were successful. Thank you Lord!

Once again, I was blessed to see my face in the mirror without glasses. But this time while I was looking at my face in the mirror, I noticed something I had not noticed before—bags under my eyes. I was like, "Wow! What happened here? When did this happen?" These eye bags were hiding behind my thick lenses all this time. I wondered for how long? Surprise, surprised! I wasn't expecting to see that. Lol!

Now let's talk about two of my not favorite topics, perimenopause and menopause. We really have to talk about this for a "hot" minute. Get it? Lol! Anyway, I don't know about you, but growing up I had only heard of menopause, never heard of perimenopause. In my late 30s, I was forgetting stuff and I really mean forgetting stuff to the point my husband was worried and concerned about our son's and my safety. I was worried and concerned too. I was forgetting the stove on, to pick up my son at the swimming pool, all kinds of things. To make matters even worse, I was irritable, everything bothered me, and I was miserable. Although my husband was worried, he was loving and supportive the whole time, and kept a watchful eye on me.

I didn't know what was going on, but I knew something I couldn't explain was happening. For the first time in my life, I felt I lost control of me. That was so scary. One day I was frustrated and was venting to Gwen, my sister-friend. I was telling her all the stuff that was happening. She listened attentively then said, "Debbie, coincidentally I was reading about perimenopause. It sounds like that's what you have." This was my first time hearing of such thing named perimenopause. She suggested to me to make an appointment with my OB/GYN and get tested for it.

After we talked, I immediately Googled perimenopause. After reading the symptoms, I knew right then that's what I was going through. I went to see my OB/GYN and told her my symptoms. She sent me to get lab work done and the results confirmed that I was going through perimenopause. This might sound odd to you, but that was the best news ever. What I was experiencing had a name. Yeah! I was not losing my mind. Double yeah! What a relief. Let me tell you, it makes a difference when you find out that the unknown has a name and that others are going through the same thing too. Misery loves company!

Coincidentally, other women at work started talking with me about their frustrations and concerns and it all sounded familiar. I told them the same thing Gwen told me and shared with them that I was going through perimenopause and they might be too. Guess what? They got tested and they too were in perimenopause. I think it was at least six of us going through perimenopause.

We bonded and formed a group. We'd meet for lunch to share our experiences, laugh, and support each other. We looked forward to our lunches and we talked about the things we forgot to remember. That was our inside joke. This made it not so bad after all.

Perimenopause transitioned into menopause. So, for the past 10 years I've been in menopause. The hot flashes just won't go away! I keep asking God, how much longer? If you are in perimenopause or menopause, I know you know exactly what I'm talking about. If you have not gotten to this point yet, you will, mark my words. Or if you are done with it, I can't wait to be where you are. This has surely been a "hot" journey! Whew!

This is the last thing I'm going to share with you. I've never had skin problems, except for that one time when I was in my mid 20s when my face broke out. I went to an esthetician and she took care of it. A few years ago, I had a burning sensation around my neck and a rash appeared there and on the left side of my abdomen. I went to see my primary care physician and she prescribed a cream that helped.

In 2019, out of the blue, a rash appeared under both breasts. The area was itchy, burning, red, raw, painful; it felt horrible. I went to the dermatologist and he said it was eczema. I was like, "Eczema! I've never had eczema." He said that as you age, your skin changes. He prescribed a cream that dried it up after a few days, but this was only temporary. The rash under my breasts kept coming back and spreading to other parts of my body. And I don't know what is causing it. It's annoying!

I've been praying to God to heal me completely, supernaturally or through medical means. I changed dermatologists to see if she could find the root cause and give me a treatment that would give me a permanent solution or keep it under control. While I was waiting to see the new dermatologist, things got so bad that I had to go see my new primary care doctor and he prescribed a cream that really worked. I did see the new dermatologist and she did a biopsy. The result was atopic dermatitis. I'm glad it wasn't anything more serious. I don't take any pills, thank God, but I use different creams on different parts of my body. That's why I always say, everybody has something going on. So, don't envy others because you don't know what they're going through.

Here is the thing, when you are going to a physician and you don't feel comfortable for whatever reason and/or not seeing good results or any improvement, then change physicians until you find one that will give you the attention your condition requires, finds out what's wrong, and recommends effective treatments.

I'll tell you that every phase of my life has brought a new challenge, always something. That's life! Somethings are harder than others to cope with or get over and sometimes life gets overwhelming. But you know what? God has been with me through it all and gotten me through each one. I rise and shine every day, with God's help. He keeps me sane, joyful, peaceful, thankful, hopeful, and going. YAY!

I try to take care of my body the best way I can. I pay attention to it and if something does not feel or look right, I get it taken care of promptly before it becomes an issue or gets worse. Despite all I've gone through and I'm going through—I know many have gone through worse things—I still look and feel good in my body and wear it well. I hope you look and feel the same in your body. If not, you sure can.

So, why did I share all of that with you? Because I want you to know that if you're going through something, you're not alone. As I said before, we are all going through something and if we're not right now, we have or will. That's just the way life goes. You will not go through this life without going through something.

Even women who look like all is good, trust me, all is not good all the time. You just never know what people are going through. I've been blessed to have many awesome, strong, resilient women through my life. Women just like you, who have been through a lot and are going through a lot. Sometimes they need someone to talk to freely and openly about things on their mind, things they are going through. Someone they trust and know genuinely cares and wouldn't judge or put their business out there. And that has been me. I always say, I'm not here to judge, I'm here to love and pray. I leave the judging to God.

Empathy, listening and giving Godly counsel are three of my God-given gifts. Alleluia! I'm humbled and thankful to God for using me in this special way. Our God-given gifts are not for us to keep, they are to give, bless, and help others. I pray that you also have someone in your life that you can talk to. It's important to talk and get things off your mind. You will feel so much better, and many times talking helps you see the light at the end of the tunnel. It will help you see things clearer, from a different perspective, explore options and solutions and make the right decisions. I've seen this happen over and over again and it has happened to me. That's why I'm a strong believer and advocate about talking to someone.

Ever since I rededicated my life to God, I talk to Him about everything and anything and He tells me what to do and who to go to, if needed. I also talk to my husband, my best friend. He is a good listener, gives great advice and we pray together. Through my adult years I've always had someone to talk to, my mom, my older sister Andrea and older friends. Since living in the U.S., I talk to Gwen when I need to talk because sometimes you just want to talk to another woman. She is my spiritual big sister. She is filled with Godly wisdom and she is a prayer warrior. I can talk to her openly and freely about everything and anything. I remember four occasions when I needed to talk. She listened attentively and gave me the best advice ever. I still use them and have shared them with others.

My dear, there may be things you're dealing with, things on your mind. Maybe you are unhappy with the way you look or feel or going through body changes or having health issues or experiencing certain discomforts. Or maybe you are facing other challenges. There will be times you feel like a failure, sad, uncertain, frustrated, desperate, depressed, imperfect or anxious. Not understanding and asking God, "Why me?" I understand; I've been there. Please know, you're not alone. We all have bad days and bad things happen; every one of us do, trust me.

It is normal to feel certain emotions when it seems like everything that could go wrong is going wrong, that everything around you is falling apart, is upside down. But what you don't want is for those feelings to linger for too long and build up. That's why it's so important to talk to someone (i.e., mom, dad, sister, brother, girlfriend, mentor, teacher, coach, pastor) or seek professional help when things are not okay.

Trust God and believe that things will turn around for good and will get better. Remember, God loves you and He is always with you even when you don't feel Him. God, through Jesus, will get you through whatever you're going through because Greater is Jesus in you. Say this right now and believe it in your heart: Greater is Jesus in Me! Pray and trust God!

"Do not be afraid or discouraged, for the Lord will personally go ahead of you. He will be with you; he will never fail you nor abandon you."

Deuteronomy 31:8 (NLT)

"...Weeping may last through the night, but joy comes with the morning."

Psalm 30:5 (NLT)

"And we know that God causes everything to work together for the good of those who love God and are called according to his purpose for them."

Romans 8:28 (NLT)

"But you belong to God, dear children. You have already won a victory over those people, because the Spirit who lives in you is greater than the spirit who lives in the world."

1 John 4:4 (NLT)

To Each Her Own

Y ou don't have to like what I like, and I don't have to like what you like. Or you don't have to do what I do, and I don't have to do what you do. And you know what? That's okay. If you are a vegan and I like eating meat, that's okay. If you like wearing makeup and I don't, that's okay too. If I like wearing dresses and you prefer pants, that's so okay. To each her own!

We all have our likes, styles and ways, and that's really okay. However, there are some women, I'm not saying you, who like to impose their likes, styles, and ways on others. And want others to be like them and do what they are doing. And when other women are not liking what they like and doing what they do or wearing what they wear or going along with them, then they criticize, shame and make them feel like something is wrong with them. This is so not right! In my opinion, that's really borderline bullying.

If you are doing this, you really need to stop because that's not nice. You would not like this done to you, right? On the other hand, if you are on the receiving end, just be who you are and don't feel pressured to be who you are not just to fit in and please others. Don't go along just to get along. It's not worth it because you are worth much more than losing you and conforming to others. The bottom line is this: Be who you are and let others be who they are. If they can't accept you the way you are, then you may need to part ways. And that's okay.

We are all unique, thank God. And you are entitled to be you and do your own thing without worrying about what others are saying or thinking. Girl, life is just too short for all this. You need to focus on what's important—your mental, emotional, and physical wellbeing. And of course, you should care for others' wellbeing too. And part of caring for others' wellbeing is not causing unnecessary stress to others. You should accept others as they are and treat them right.

Let's use our energy in positive ways to uplift, encourage, and build up each other, and not in negative ways to degrade, discourage, and tear down each other. Let's love, treat each other with dignity, respect, and decency. Let's celebrate each other and accept who we are as individuals.

> *"Dear children, let's not merely say that we love each other; let us show the truth by our action."*
>
> *1 John 3:18 (NLT)*

Be You! Do You! But Who Are You?

L et who you are rise and shine! Be you and do you! Why would you want to be someone other than yourself? You are uniquely beautiful, filled with gifts, ideas, creativity, emotions, etc. You have personality traits no one else has, and certain qualities and expressions that are yours only. You have your own way of thinking and doing things. You have your unique fashion or no fashion, signature style or no style at all. But you know what? That's just who you are!

Some people might love those things about you while others might not and that's okay because everybody is entitled to feel however they want to feel. But don't allow that to affect you or make you feel bad. The truth is, you can't please everybody, and you shouldn't feel obligated to do so or feel bad about it. Is there room for improvement? Always! But anything you decide to do or not do, do it because you want to, not because you feel forced. pressured or obligated.

However, there are two things you should always want to do, which are, treat everybody with respect and with dignity because everybody deserves that. Likewise, those are the two things you should expect from others. This will surely make our world a better place for all if we all did these two simple but yet powerful things.

"Do to others as you would like them to do to you."

Luke 6:31 (NLT)

As long as what you are doing is not detrimental or harmful to you or others, be you and do you. But for you to be you and do you, you really have to love you and know who you are. Otherwise, how can you be you and do you? So, we're right back to what I've been saying all along. You have to know who you are. So, who are you? Can you answer that? Do you really know who you are?

Allow me to ask you a few questions and see how much you know you. I'll give you my answers.

- What are you passionate about? I'm passionate about doing whatever God tells me to do and helping people.
- What do you love about you? I love my smile. I think it is welcoming, warm and beautiful, just like my mom's.
- What's one of your strengths? Listening. I give people my undivided attention and I genuinely care and empathize, and I help them see the best in them.
- What's one of your weaknesses? I have absolutely no sense of direction. I get lost easily.
- What do you dislike? I don't like name calling. I feel it is demeaning because words matter.
- What's your favorite color? Fuchsia is my favorite color.
- What's your pet peeve? One of my pet peeves is when people take credit for others' work.

So, how did you do?

There's one thing I've noticed over the years when talking with women, they don't know who they are or know their worth. They don't even know the little things about themselves. When I've asked certain questions, they can't answer. They give me the deer in headlights look. And they have a hard time saying good things about themselves. I practically have to drag it out of their mouths. I'm like, really! Somehow, they think that saying good things about themselves is a bad thing. But these same women don't think it twice to say all kinds of negative things about themselves. And I walk away feeling sad and thinking, you don't know your worth. And I ask myself, what can I do to make her see the greatness in her and feel good about herself?

Hopefully, you know who you are and your worth and feel good about yourself and say good things about yourself. There is absolutely nothing wrong with any of that as long as you're not doing it to put someone else down or feel superior. Knowing who you are and recognizing the good things in you is a good thing. It sure is! This will boost your self-esteem and self-confidence. It will help you make good decisions in all aspects of your life. It will help you when choosing a life partner, friends, profession, career, etc. Celebrate who you are! When you know who you are, you will be you and do you and not worry about what other people say or think about you or wait for others to validate you.

I've known who I am for a long time and loving every bit of me. The way I see it, if you don't like who I am, that's not my problem, it's yours. I'm definitely not trying to be anyone else or impress anyone. I'm just being me and doing me. I'm not comparing or copying anyone and certainly not trying to compete with anyone. So not worth it.

Honestly, I really don't look on other women's fashions and styles. I do me! I like to feel and look beautiful in my own way. Don't get me wrong, I admire other women's unique beauty, fashions, and styles and I give compliments all the time. However, I have my own personal style and I'm comfortable with it whether it's in style or not.

Girlfriend, find your own and be uniquely you. Have your own personal style and unique fashion and feel confident, comfortable and uniquely beautiful. Be you and do you! Also, when you have your own personal style, you're not jumping on every trend and following the crowd.

For example, during fall and winter I love wearing

bold colorful fun socks with pants, jeans and sweat pants with my low cut/ankle boots or Easy Spirit Travel Time clogs. I get compliments about my socks all the time; they are so colorful and eye catching. And if I didn't get compliments, that'd be okay too. During summer and spring, I love wearing my anklets, they are so cute.

I'd like you to take a moment to think about this.

- Who are you?
- Are you being you and doing you?
- What is your personal style, unique fashion, something that is uniquely yours? That's all you!

Love and feel good about who you are. Be you and do you!

Know What Looks Great on You

⌒⌒⌒

I think most women want to look their best when heading out into the world. When you look in the mirror before heading out to wherever you're going, are you happy with the way you look? Be honest. Do you think, "I look okay. I don't like how I look. This is as good as it gets." Or "I look great! I'm loving it! I feel beautiful! I look fabulous!"

When you look your best, you will then feel sure of yourself and not need validation from others. Absolutely, compliments are welcome and appreciated, but when you don't get any, you're still okay and can go about your daily business happily and with confidence.

In this life there are things we can and can't control. The good thing is that looking your best is one of those things you can control. You can control how you look. You decide your look. So, the key to nailing your best, most attractive, and beautiful look is knowing what looks great on you, i.e., hairstyles, hair colors, makeup, clothes, shoes, jewelry, accessories, handbags, etc.

Therefore, another way of knowing you, is knowing what looks great on you, what flatters you best, enhances your natural beauty—what brings out the best you. In other words, what you wear matters! Therefore, you want to wear clothes that fit your body type, and makes you look and feel great. The right fitting clothes will make the difference; you feel comfortable, confident, and empowered. The truth is, what may look great on you may not look so great on me and vice versa, and that's okay. To each her own! Wear what looks great on you.

You want to wear clothes that accentuate your best features and minimize or hide your flaws. Honestly, you don't have to (and really shouldn't) settle for ill-fitting clothes. We are so blessed to live in an age where there are designs and styles made to fit every body shape, size and height, and not have to settle for less. Woo hoo!

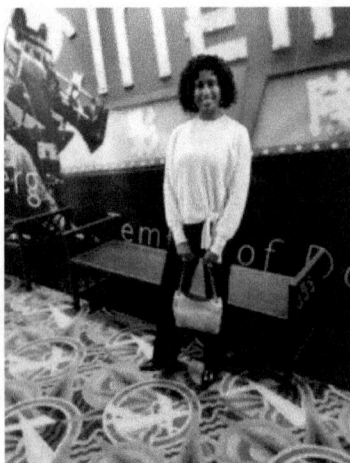

Knowing your body shape and flaws is important. We all have flaws; we just have to work with what we have. I know my body shape and flaws; therefore, I know what looks great on me and what doesn't. I'm 5'5 ½". I have long legs and short torso, so I buy tall in pants even though sometimes it maybe a little too long and need altering, but regular is definitely too short. And I love wide-legged pants. I think they nicely accentuate my long legs. Also, I've always had a protruding tummy and it's not going anywhere. I don't like anything fitted or clingy over my tummy. Therefore, I like fabrics to fall softly or loosely drape over it. And this style hides my tummy to the point that you can't even notice it.

I like my clothes to fit loosely. I select clothes that look and feel great on me because not every fashion or style looks or feels great. Some clothes just don't fit right and I won't wear them just because they are the latest fashion trend. I'm not driven by fashion trends or brand names, I'm driven by what looks and feels great on my body (perfect fit, style, color). I prefer simple and timeless fashion trends that never go out of style. That's just me.

- Do you know what looks great on you?

- Have you taken the time to know your body type?
- Do you dress for your body shape?
- What styles do you like or don't like?
- What styles brings out your best, makes you look beautiful and feel awesome?

There are many articles about how to dress for your body type. Take time to learn how to select the right cuts, patterns, styles and fabrics that will work for your body type and gives you your best look. Have fun beautifying you!

Try a New Look

Girlfriend, sometimes we just need a new look. Sometimes it is just time to try something new. A new look is an instant morale, self-confidence and self-esteem booster and it is so much fun. I know the first time it is scary but just do it. You will be okay! When you look at yourself in the mirror, you will be like, oh wow… I look amazing! You will feel so good and you will want to keep doing it. Lol!

So, come on girl, take your "me time" and pamper yourself. Surprise yourself and others with "your new look" and have fun with it. Let's get right to it…

New Haircut—New Hairstyle—New Color—Rock Your Gray

If you want to change your look, changing your haircut, hairstyle, and hair color will do the trick. Some women stick to one haircut, one hairstyle, and one color and that's fine. But if you want to change your look, don't be afraid, go for it! Go to your hairstylist and tell her/him you want a new look and ask her/him for suggestions. Then just do it!

Also, there are women who want to stop coloring their hair but don't do it because they are not ready to embrace their gray hair and they fear it will make them look older. Well, lately I've seen women (and younger women too) rock their gray hair and they look amazing. Your hairstylist can give you tips to keep your gray hair looking healthy, pretty and shiny and recommend a few cute haircuts and hairstyles that will fit your face, hair texture, and make you look beautiful.

Over the years I've had my share of haircuts, hairstyles, and colors when my hair was natural and relaxed (straightened). I really enjoy trying different things just to look different. While living in Panama I had the best hairstylist, Dawn. My hair looked fabulous all the time.

In my early 50s, I stopped coloring my hair and rocked my gray hair for a few years. I made sure it had a nice gray tone and was shiny. Then I started back coloring my hair. I do it myself. My hairstylist, Monah, did my relaxer. I let my hair grow out a bit to give me the flexibility to do different simple hair styles. Now with COVID-19, I stopped relaxing my hair. It's natural and I have a Teenie Weenie Afro (TWA) and I'm loving it.

Sometimes a new look is what you need to perk up, give you a boost, make you feel better about yourself and build your self-confidence. A new look makes you feel and look more attractive and beautiful. It makes you feel alive!

Hairpieces and Wigs

Do you want to change your look and look fabulous without the hassle? Hairpieces and wigs will do the trick. I've always been surrounded by women (young and old) who wore different hairpieces and wigs and they looked

fabulous. They changed their look all the time. You never knew who was going to show up. One of the things that surprised me was that most of the women had a full head of hair. So, I asked them why they wore wigs and hairpieces? They said, "It's so easy!" It gave them the flexibility to rock a new look with different hairstyles, lengths, and colors without damaging or messing with their hair.

I was never interested in hairpieces or wigs until 2018. I was looking for a simple, low maintenance hairstyle and I said to myself, "Why not pull back my hair and wear a bun?" I never wore a hair bun until September 2018 when I bought my first bun and thereafter bought a few more. Every time I'd go to Grace Beauty Supply 3 LLC, DD the owner and my friend, would ask me, "How many of these you need?" Lol!

Then I decided to venture into trying other hair pieces and a wig to change my look. I thought, since my hair is thinning, why not get a new look without damaging the little hair I have because, as you know, there are some hair styles that break your hair. And it seemed like every other woman I knew was rockin' a hair piece or wig. The truth is, I couldn't tell if it was a wig or their own hair unless they told me.

I bought and wore my first wig in January 2019 and I looked younger, beautiful, and fabulous and it felt good on my head. I got so many compliments, it was surreal. I have to give credit to Sandra, "The Wig Boss," my co-worker. I had mentioned to her that I was looking for a wig that would fit my face. She found the perfect one and texted it to me. After I got the wig, she shaped it and the rest is history.

Sometimes you just need to change things up a bit and surprise yourself and others. You just have to be daring and try something new, a new look. I've bought a few more wigs. Different styles, lengths, colors and they all give me a fresh, different and new look. I'm having so much fun and loving it! You should try it too.

Hairpieces and wigs have come a long way and some look so natural. There are synthetic and human hair wigs and hairpieces. They come in a ton of different styles, colors and lengths, and a range of prices. Much to choose

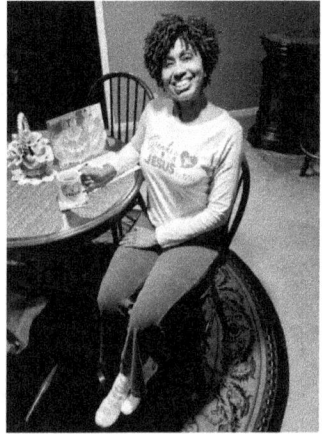

from but do your research. It really boils down to your preference and how much you want to spend. But I'm telling you, it gives you flexibility and it is so much fun!

You can also have your hairstylist cut and style your wigs and hairpieces for you. Like everything else, there is a right way to put on wigs so not to damage your hair. You will definitely want to read and follow instructions on how to care for them so they look good and last.

There are also different accessories to secure them on your head. You don't want your hairpiece or wig falling off or becoming lop-sided. I've seen lop-sided wigs; not a pretty sight. Also, hairpieces and wigs are a great solution for thinning or damaged hair, hair loss, or when going through medical treatments/issues that cause hair loss such as chemotherapy, alopecia, etc.

- Do you want a new look?
- Have you tried a new look lately?
- Do you want to change your look?
- Have you thought about it?

If you haven't thought about a new look, there is no better time than now to be adventurous and try a new look. Go for it! Surprise yourself, your family and friends with a new you. Just do it! You go, girl!

Total Body Care

Total Body Care from Head to Toe

~⊙⊙~

G irlfriend, creams and lotions have to be your skin's best friend, especially as you age. They will hydrate your skin and make it look and stay healthy, younger looking, slow down the wrinkling process, and preserve it for a longer time than if you use nothing. The earlier you start to incorporate creams and lotions into your skincare regimen, the better it will be for your skin because you are pre-conditioning and pre-maintaining your skin. That will help you in the long run as you age.

As we all know, the skin is the body's largest organ and is different depending on the part of the body. Likewise, the skin treatment and products will be different. Also, the skin areas we usually cover are more protected than the skin areas that are exposed; therefore, this too must be considered when choosing your skincare products.

Skincare from head to toe is important because it helps keep your skin healthy, moist, and age beautifully and gracefully. You really have to take care of your skin, it's the only one you have and you want to keep it in the best condition

for as long as possible.

Now I'll share with you my skincare regimen, tips and the products I use to keep my skin looking healthy, beautiful, and glowing. And no, I'm not getting paid by anyone to promote their products. I've used all of the products I'll be talking about. Some of these products I've used for many years and had great results that are noticeable to me and others. I'm all about results!

The best part is that the skincare products I use work for me, are affordable, and last a long time. You might be already using some of the products and having great results just like me, and if you're not using them, you might consider trying them. Remember, every product doesn't work for every skin type (i.e., normal, oily, dry, combination, sensitive) and sometimes you have to keep trying until you find the right one for your skin. The key is how easily a product is absorbed and how it feels on your skin.

Only you know your skin and its history. And only you know what feels good on your skin and if you see improvements over time. If your skincare regimen is working for you, stick with it. If it is not or you don't have one or just want to add or try something new, my tips will be helpful. Whatever your case may be, you will still get something out of this.

With the constant barrage of skincare infomercials, it is so easy to become a product junkie and wind up spending a fortune. That's why I really try not to look at skincare infomercials because it's easy for me to get hooked, and find myself ordering stuff, then regretting it later. Has this happened to you?

I do like mixing things up so you will notice that I use different brands. Whatever feels good on my skin, gives good results, and is affordable, that's what I use.

I'm also going to give you tips about total body care from head to toe, maintenance, grooming and hygiene because our whole body needs our undivided attention and our TLC. We want our skin and whole body to look and feel healthy and beautiful, age gracefully, and smell fresh. We sure do! I told you, we are going to talk about everything and I mean everything. So hold on tight! Here we go!

Hair and Scalp

At this stage of my life, I really try to keep things simple. As I mentioned before, I wanted a hairstyle that was simple, manageable, and looked good on me. As I've gotten older, my hair grayed, the texture changed, and it thinned. Therefore, I am very selective about hairstyles because not every hairstyle looks good on me, and even worse, it might damage my hair.

When I was younger, I didn't mind going to the salon weekly, but now that I'm older, I just can't do it. Sitting three to five hours every week in a salon and knowing I have things to do (clean house, laundry, grocery shopping, run errands, etc.) was stressing me out. Not only that, just sitting and waiting hours for my turn and knowing that what was to be done should only take one to one and a half hours and not three to five hours was frustrating.

When you have a full-time job, every minute counts. Moreover, professional hair care can get expensive. I don't have that kind of money to spend on my hair every week when I have bills to pay. That's just me. As I said before, to each her own.

Anyway, every eight to10 weeks I used to get my hair straightened with a relaxer and took care of my hair in between. My hairstylist, Monah, is awesome with respecting her client's time. She'd have me in and out. What I love about her is that she doesn't double, triple book. That worked for me. Then she moved to another salon and accommodated me by coming to my home. That started January 18, 2020. Well, it didn't last long. My second appointment, March 14, 2020, was our last one due to COVID-19. So, I let my hair grow out but then it started to break and was looking bad. I decided to cut it off and had my son shape it into a nice TWA. I must say it looks pretty good. I've gotten many compliments.

When I had a relaxer and now natural, I color my hair with Clairol Professional Beautiful Collection advanced gray solution, semi-permanent color, 2RV Burgundy Brown and 2A Rich Dark Brown. I leave a gray patch, just like my mom. I don't mix the two colors before applying. I have my own way of applying them to my hair. I can attest that these products really cover the gray, the colors lasts for more than eight weeks, and they don't damage your hair. I've gotten so many compliments, even from Monah. Anytime I'd get my relaxer, she'd ask me if I had done it recently because it still looked good.

I use two shampoos. I have dry scalp and to prevent flaking I first shampoo twice with Selsun Blue, Itchy Dry Scalp, Extra Hydrating Formula, Dandruff Shampoo Plus. Then I shampoo once with Motions Moisture Lavish Shampoo, which leaves my hair soft, silky, and moisturized. My dear girlfriend, Angie, who died a few years ago, introduced me to Motions products. These are great products. I towel dry my hair and condition.

I alternate between different conditioners, but the ones I like the most are Dr. Miracle's Super Strength Deep Conditioner, Motions Moisture Plus Conditioner, DOO GRO, Shea Moisture Raw Shea Butter Moisture Recovery Treatment, Olive Oil Replenishing Conditioner, Argan Oil Intensive Conditioning Treatment, Silk Elements Conditioner and Palmer's Coconut Oil Formula, repairing conditioner. I apply the conditioner as directed. Then I apply Shea Moisture Jamaican Black Castor Oil Strengthen & Restore Leave-in Conditioner from root to ends and massage in my scalp. As you can clearly see, I'm trying to keep the little hair I have on my head.

After I've applied the leave-in conditioner, I section my hair and apply Isoplus Castor Oil Hair & Scalp Conditioner to my scalp and massage in gently through my hair. Then I apply a small amount of Soft & Beautiful Botanicals, Lite Crème Moisturizer to my damp hair to activate my natural curls and let it air dry.

A healthy hair and healthy scalp go hand in hand. Hair is super important to most women and many spend a whole lot of money and time to keep it healthy and looking beautiful. That's because we know our hair is an eye catcher, just like our eyebrows.

As you already know, we all have different hair types and textures. And we do different things to our hair, such as coloring, using relaxers, blow drying, using a curling iron, etc. and when not done properly, these things can potentially weaken or damage our hair and cause scalp issues. Then we might have dry scalp, dandruff or other issues, and depending on the severity, may require medical care. This is why hair and scalp care and treatment varies and should be customized to individual needs.

Also, we trust and depend on our hair stylist to give our scalp and hair the best care and treatment, and give recommendations on how to keep and maintain our hair so it's healthy and gorgeous. Our stylist will also recommend flattering hairstyles and haircuts that will make us look our best, younger, glamourous and perform miracles at times. And there are some of us who do our own hair or do as much as we can to the best of our abilities. But here's the deal, as long as you have healthy scalp and hair, and you are happy with both, that's what counts. Be you and do you!

Okay, so let's talk for a minute.

- What's your scalp and hair care regime? Is it working for you? If it's working for you, awesome. If it's not, have you done anything about it or planning to do something about it?
- Have you talked with your hairstylist or done your own research?
- Are your scalp and hair healthy? Are you having any issues? If you are having issues, have you been to a doctor? If not, you may really want to consider going and getting this taken care of sooner than later. Okay.

Face

Having an effective face skincare plan and using products that work for your skin are keys to healthy skin and to aging beautifully and gracefully. I have a face skincare routine and products that work for me. And I really do a good job at not touching my face, that's why I've not had any breakouts in years. That really helps.

If you go bare-face like me, au naturel, then set your skin up for success by using the right products, for your skin type, that give you the best results. Use products that will keep your skin hydrated, looking healthy, radiant, and beautiful.

Daily—morning and bedtime—I gently cleanse my face with lukewarm water and Aveeno Clear Complexion Foaming Cleanser, no scrubbing. I've been using the Aveeno foaming cleanser for about 20 years and I love it, because it leaves my face feeling soft, clean and fresh and not dry.

In the morning after I've cleansed my face and pat dried gently, I apply L'Oréal Collagen moisture filler. I've been using it since fall 2017 and I love how it makes my skin feel. It is lightweight and non-greasy. It leaves my skin feeling soft, plump, and younger looking and the best part is that it is surprisingly inexpensive. This is the one product I apply every time after I cleanse my face.

I also apply a dab of Vaseline Petroleum Jelly on my eyebrows, glabella, and the outside of my nose, because those areas get a little dry and flaky at times especially during the winter. I also apply it on my chin because it is a little bumpy from ingrown hairs. In the winter I also apply a thicker moisturizer, Nivea Cream. Then I apply a dab of Spring Valley Vitamin E Skin Oil and gently rub on my face.

When I'm going out, the last product I apply is Neutrogena Age Shield sunscreen SPF 110. Although I knew the importance of sunscreen, I had not made it a part of my skincare routine until January 2019. Go figure! I really never liked being directly in the sun so I'm rarely in it. I believe that helped me. I recommend to make sunscreen a part of your skincare routine. Don't leave home without it! It so happens that the product I use has a SPF of 110 but based on what I've read, 50 SPF is as good.

At night after I've cleansed my face with Aveeno Clear Complexion Foaming Cleanser and pat dried gently, I apply L'Oréal Collagen moisture filler, then the Neutrogena Rapid Wrinkle Repair serum followed by Neutrogena Ageless Intensive Anti-Wrinkle deep wrinkle night moisturizer.

I'm trying out two eye creams but I'm not going to list the names because the jury is still out. I started using these products since fall 2019.

March 15, 2020, I was channel surfing and wound up watching the Meaningful Beauty informational. Cindy Crawford was promoting new products and she got my attention. Let me be clear, I'm still using the products I mentioned before and still seeing great results. Anyway, I wound up ordering the Special Offer, which was at a great price that included five products plus three free gifts. I tried all of the products. They all felt great on my skin.

Since I was already using great products and having great results, I really didn't need all of the Meaningful Beauty products. I really liked the Youth Activating Melon Serum, Anti-Aging Day Crème and the Age Recovery Night Crème with Melon Extract & Retinol. So I've added them to my beauty regimen. Now I alternate between products.

After trying different skincare products, these work for me. If you don't have a skincare regimen, I encourage you to do so. Research and learn why skincare is important especially as we age, and look for the best skincare products for your skin type. I suggest you learn the right way and the correct order to apply face skincare products to get the best results because there is a right way and correct order to apply the different types of products. You will feel the difference in the way your skin absorbs the products, how your skin feels, and it will make a noticeable difference.

At the beginning I really was not paying attention to the way and the order in which I applied the products until one day I read about it and started following the application guide on the products. You really need to read all of the instructions and follow them if you want the best results.

Sometimes we don't get or see the results we expect, and get disappointed, because we're not reading and following instructions. I'm talking to myself too. Also, read other related skincare topics because there is always something new to learn.

Do you want your skin to look healthy, radiant, and beautiful and keep the wrinkles away for as long as possible? I know you do! We all do! Of course, genetics play a role in aging and there are other factors but one thing we can do is help ourselves as much as possible.

So, do you have a face skin care regimen? If yes, is it working for you?

Are you happy with it? If you don't have one, have you thought about it? If no, this is a good time to think about it, shop around and start your face skin care regimen.

Facials

On weekends, I do my own facials. I alternate with different products. I do a facial scrub with Queen Helene Mint Julep Scrub or Queen Helene Cocoa Butter. I then exfoliate with Tree Hut Shea Sugar Scrub Coconut Lime. This scrub leaves my face so soft. Then I apply one of my Queen Helene facial masques (Mint Julep Masque, Mud Pack Masque or Grape Seed Peel-off Masque), which I've been using for at least eight years. I order these from Amazon. Then I apply one of my Earth Therapeutics facial sheet masks (Soothing Aloe Vera Mask, Retinol, Vitamin E or Rejuvenating Collagen Mask), which I started using Fall 2018. These are fabulous and your face feels great! I buy them from Kohl's. All of these facial products are so affordable and effective.

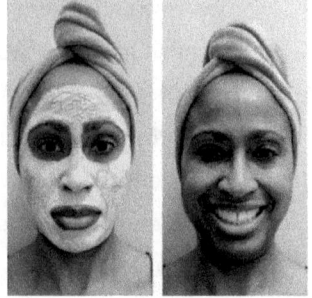

When I lived in Panama and I was in my late 20s, I don't know what happened, but my skin broke out horribly. I never had a breakout as a teenager then this happened. I had to do something about it. So, I started professional facial treatments with the best esthetician at the Estee Lauder Institute. At the beginning, if I remember correctly, I had facial treatments every two weeks. When my face got back to normal, I continued monthly. Never had a problem after that.

When I came to the U.S., I somehow forgot about professional facial massage and treatment. As I got older, I thought, I probably need to get back to getting professional facial massages and treatments to reap all of the benefits, such as deep cleansing, exfoliation and hydration. Girlfriend, every part of a facial massage treatment feels so good and relaxing, It feels like heaven! YAY!

I really don't know why I didn't continue getting professional facial massages and treatments when I moved to the U.S., especially when I noticed changes in my skin due to seasonal changes. Well, better late than never. So now I'm doing everything within my means to keep my skin in the best possible condition and help it age healthfully, beautifully and gracefully.

The truth is that no matter what or how much I do at home, it's not the same as getting it done professionally, every so often. It's a little pricy and finding time to get it done when there is not enough time, is challenging. That's why when I started again December 1, 2017, I decided that I'd do it twice a year, max four times, if I can fit it in.

I try to schedule facial massages and treatments on special occasions, like my birthday and Christmas. This is my "me time" to treat and pamper myself. It took me a while to find the perfect place to get the best service, great ambience, and feel relaxed and comfortable. I finally found it, Stafford Massage and Healing Arts, but due to coronavirus they had temporarily closed. Sherry is my esthetician. She is fabulous!

If you haven't had a professional facial treatment yet, you really don't know what you're missing. You really should try it. They offer different types of facials and can customize them based on your skin type and any specific needs and they will give you recommendations. Most important, your face will feel and look refreshed, revived, and glowing. I know, it's a little pricy and most of us don't have the time to fit this in, but if you can afford it and need "me time," go for it. We all deserve a little pampering. Go get a facial!

Also, if you want to do the couple massage package or go with a girlfriend or girlfriends, this is perfect. My husband and I have done the couples therapeutic body massage to celebrate our wedding anniversary. When you're there you feel like you're in another world. The aroma and the ambience is welcoming, soothing, and so relaxing. I'm right now on a pause due to coronavirus, but I'm looking forward to getting a professional facial massage and treatment in the near future. I miss my facials!

In January 2019, I started doing my own facial massages. I started doing them a couple times a week, but now it's whenever I remember. I watch and follow Abigail James Anti-Aging, Face lifting massage YouTube video. She is awesome! I like her videos. She is very knowledgeable. She informs, instructs, and she's easy to follow. She's just too cool! I find that the facial massage boosts my circulation and makes my face look gorgeous with a natural flush. I apply oil on my face so that my fingers gently glide on my skin when massaging it.

Doing my own facial massage feels so good. But as I mentioned before, getting a professional facial massage, feels even better.

Makeup

I'm really not into makeup. I don't like how it feels on my face. In my 20s and 30s, I wore light makeup to work and church and then stepped it up a notch when going to parties or events. Over the years, having to factor in makeup time in the mornings when going to work got to be a little too much and I'll admit I got a little lazy too. I occasionally wear makeup to work and when I'm going to church, on special occasions, and photo shoots for my Christian online magazine.

For the past 20 years, I've been pretty much makeup free. For this reason face skincare is important to me. I want my skin to be healthy, clean, well-rested, fresh, smooth, moisturized, and look radiant. I want to look naturally beautiful without makeup and I do. I want to achieve my best looking version at any age. I think I'm doing pretty good thus far. Of course with God's help. YAY!

When I do put on makeup it is mainly concealer, face powder, blush, eyebrow pencil, lip pencil liner, and lipstick. I don't wear eye makeup because my eyes are very sensitive. The products I use are: Covergirl+Olay Concealer Balm Fair Light under my eyes, upper lip area and chin (dark spots due to tweezing); Covergirl Trublend Pressed Powder Translucent Tawny on my face; Revlon Powder Blush Smoky Rose on my cheeks; pencil lip liner (various brands/colors to match lipstick); Revlon Super Lustrous Lipstick (variety of colors); Mary Kay Nourishine Plus Lip Gloss (variety of colors) that matches lipstick; and black eyebrow pencil (any brand) to cover gray hairs and fill in my eyebrows.

I've used these products for years and they've served me well. When I wear makeup, it enhances my look and brings out my natural beauty. All these products are reputable and the best part, affordable.

There are some women who have mastered the art of putting on makeup, accentuating their best features, perfectly concealing their flaws, and looking beautifully fabulous. Your best look is what you want to achieve and that's exactly what they do. You can't help but look at them and say "Oh WOW!" And they love it and have fun with it.

I love to see perfectly applied makeup. I admire women who know how to do it right. It's an art! I'm talking about the eye shadow, eyelashes, eye liner, the whole works. When women want to look flawless, glamourous, and beautiful for a special occasion they hire professional makeup artists. I've had professional makeup done twice. When I looked in the mirror I was like, "WOW! Who's that girl? I look beautifully fabulous!"

I've never mastered applying makeup in that way. That's just never been my thing. To each her own! I do the basics. But the little I do, when I do it, I try to do it right. Here's the thing, if you're going to wear makeup make sure to find the right makeup colors that blend seamlessly with your skin tone, complements your skin tone, and enhances your natural beauty. It may be tricky at first but once you get it, you get it. Also, take time to learn how to put on your makeup properly. It makes a difference. Fortunately, you can find everything on the internet. So invest a little time researching and learning how to apply your makeup perfectly so you look fresh, flawless, and fabulously beautiful.

Are you a makeup kind of girl or no makeup or in between? No matter which one you are… Be you and do you!

Eyebrows

I'm old school so I keep my eyebrows shaped by plucking stray hairs with a tweezer and trimmed with small scissors. I have a few gray hairs popping in my brows. At first, I was plucking them out, but my eyebrows were getting patchy so now I use a black eyebrow pencil and slightly dab on them to darken and fill in.

Daily, I apply a little Vaseline (petroleum jelly) on my eyebrows and glabella to keep that area from getting flaky. If I don't, it will get flaky, especially during the winter.

Nowadays, women have many options to have well-shaped and attractive eyebrows, i.e., threading, waxing, tattooing, plucking, laser, tinting, microblading, and more. Make sure to research before trying any of them. There are many eyebrow products to make your eyebrows look impressive and gorgeous.

As you know, your eyebrows are one of the first things that draws attention to your face. More so now that we are wearing mask due to COVID-19. Beautiful eyebrows are attention catchers, just like your hair. Eyebrows shapes have evolved over the years. They've gone from thin to thick and in between. If you're like me, you've been messing with your eyebrows from the time you were a teenager and your eyebrows have evolved with you.

The bottom line is, you decide what you want to do or not do with your eyebrows. Your eyebrows give you your distinct look and personality. Therefore, whatever look you like or feel comfortable with, go for it. To each her own!

Skin Around Eyes

After I had my cataract surgery (July 2018), I noticed bags under my eyes. I guess they've been there for a while but I didn't notice them before because, as I mentioned earlier, I wore thick lenses and couldn't see my face without my glasses. So, this year I started placing cold compress over the area for 20 minutes to reduce the puffiness. Occasionally I watch and follow Abigail James massage to help get rid of puffy, tired eyes YouTube video. I'm not going to fool myself, I know the bags are not going anywhere. I'm just trying to make them look better or better yet, not look any worse.

My eyes are very sensitive so I'm very careful not to do too much around my eyes. Therefore, I never applied creams around my eyes. Perhaps that may have contributed to my saggy skin above my eyes and the bags under my eyes because the rest of my face is fine.

Since I noticed my bags, I started using eye creams around my eye area. I'm not giving the names of the products I've tried and currently using, because I've not seen the results they claim. The bags are still there. I will say that they don't look worse, so that's a good thing. At this point, I'm not expecting a miracle, meaning for the bags to disappear. Just trying to maintain things as they are for as long as possible. I noticed that the bags are less noticeable when I smile so I do a lot of smiling. The good thing is that I love to smile so it's no biggie.

- Is the skin around your eyes sagging?
- Do you have bags under your eyes? If yes, what are you doing about it? Or maybe it's not a big deal to you and that's fine.

Nose Hair

I don't know about you but I don't like nose hairs sticking out of my nostrils (worse yet gray hairs), so I trim my nose hairs with a small scissors at least twice a week. There are nose trimmers, which are safer to use but I've never tried any. Maybe I will one day.

Thinking about it, this is one of those topics women don't talk about. I don't recall having a conversation with any woman about nose hair, not even my mom, sisters or girlfriends. I know not all women deal with this but some of us do. It's one of those things that no matter how good you look, how well dressed you are, it is unappealing when it's not taken care of.

When nose hairs are not trimmed, it becomes a distraction to the person looking at you. You get what I mean. Absolutely, this is something we should pay attention to, especially as we get older. As we age, some things just seem to get out of control, and this is one of them. Anyway, this is an important part of grooming.

- Do you have nose hair issues? If you do, do you keep them trimmed?

• Have you been paying attention to them or you just never thought of it?

Well, this is a good time to start paying attention and keeping them groomed.

Ears

Daily, when I moisturize my face and neck, I also moisturize my ears with my facial creams and with Vaseline Petroleum Jelly because my ears are part of my face. I'll be honest, I wash my ears when I shower, dry them properly and gently clean inside with Q-tips (moistened), but I didn't use to moisturize them until one day I noticed a co-worker's ears. Her ears were so dry and flaky, it was very unattractive. At that time I wondered if mine looked that way. That made me start looking at them closely and moisturizing daily.

I definitely pay more attention to my ears during the winter. Also, I keep them groomed. There are two stray hairs that pop-up on my ears every so often so I make sure to look for them and pluck them.

• Do you moisturize your ears?
• Have you ever thought of it? If you haven't, this is the perfect time to start.

Upper Lip Hair

When I went into full blown menopause, I noticed my facial hair more. Specifically, my upper lip hair was more prominent, and it bothered me. I started researching and calling around looking for ways to permanently or temporarily remove the hair. That's when I found out that there is a window to do laser hair removal and I didn't know that. Once your hair is gray, laser does not work because the laser can't detect it. Electrolysis was the option I found, but I decided not do that but I knew I needed to do something.

I went to CVS to look around and found Olay smooth finish Facial Hair Removal duo (medium to coarse hair). This product worked well and I used it for years. Then fall 2018, I was watching an informercial on television about the Finishing Touch Flawless facial hair remover and decided to buy and try. It's the best hair remover ever! It's just too easy to use and does the job. In a few minutes, the hair is totally gone, no discomfort or pain. I love it!

I'm working from home now due to COVID-19 but when I was going to work four days a week and teleworked one day a week, I'd use the Finishing Touch Flawless facial remover daily on my upper lip area. Just like how men shave every day. Now that I'm home, I do it when I'm going out or every two to three days a week. I'm telling you, this is the best hair remover product ever!

- Do you have upper lip hair?
- How are you dealing with it?
- Have you done permanent hair removal?
- Have you considered permanent hair removal? Start researching early so you know your options and can act at the appropriate time. Timing is important depending on the option you take.

Lips

When I moved to the U.S. in 1999, that was my first winter and it was a harsh one. Everything that could go wrong with my body, went wrong. My lips were dry, chapped, cracked, and bled. It was painful! My lips looked horrible, and with lipstick, they looked worse. I was self-conscious about my lips and had to find a remedy quickly. So, I prayed about it.

One day I noticed that my husband had this lip ointment, Blistex Medicated Lip Ointment. I decided to try it, and that was my answer to prayer. The following day my lips started to heal and felt so much better. Ever since then, no matter how cold it gets, I've not had dry, chapped, cracked or bleeding lips.

All year round, every morning I apply Blistex on my lips and I don't have to reapply because it works all day long. This is a great product! Great results! This is one of my miracle products I can't do without. During winter I also apply Vaseline Petroleum Jelly on my lips. This is my go-to product for many things. It is amazing!

How are you lips doing? Any issues? If yes, there are a lot of over the counter products and treatments that can help. You just have to find the right one that works for you. If the issue persists, then see your doctor.

Oral Hygiene

I love to smile; therefore, I like my teeth looking healthy, clean and bright, and my breath smelling fresh. I brush my teeth and tongue with Sensodyne Extra Whitening toothpaste for sensitive teeth and cavity prevention at least twice a day, when I wake up and before going to bed. Tongue hygiene is also important because it helps prevent bad breath.

Every day I floss (reduces gum disease and bad breath) before brushing my teeth. I like to rinse vigorously with Listerine (original) making sure it comes in contact with all areas in my mouth, then I gargle and spit it out. My mouth feels clean and smells fresh.

A couple years ago, I started using over-the-counter whitening products. I use them not because I think they will make my teeth whiter but because they make my teeth look brighter. I like the CVS Health Dissolving Whitening Strips. I use it whenever I remember.

I visit my dentist twice a year for cleaning and to take care of any cavities or any other issues. So far, so good.

Smiling has so many health benefits, I encourage you to look them up. Just think, your beautiful smile might just lighten and brighten someone's day. A smile also makes people feel welcomed, relaxed, and appreciated. Make it a point to smile more!

Bad breath is embarrassing and a turn off, so you want to make sure your breath smells fresh. Research ways to smell your own breath or ask a loved one you feel comfortable with, if your breath smells bad. Hopefully your loved one will tell you the truth whether or not you ask, even though it may be awkward and uncomfortable.

The bottom line is that you want to keep your mouth clean and fresh. However, if you have bad breath and practice good oral hygiene and it does not improve, then go see your dentist or doctor because there may be underlying conditions.

Chin Hair

With menopause, my chin hair are out of control. I find myself tweezing the coarse dark hairs and gray hairs on my chin daily, a few times through the day. They seem to grow so fast, I can't keep up with them. No, I'm not growing a beard. Lol. But, I'll tell you that I spend a lot of time plucking my chin hair.

Before I had my cataract surgery, July 2018, I was double digit nearsighted, but I could see my chin hair with a 10x magnifying mirror. Post cataract surgery, I can't see a thing near so I had to upgrade to a 20x magnifying mirror so that I can see exactly what's going on with my chin. I have a few magnifying mirrors and I carry one in my handbag just in case I need it. Lol.

Tweezing my chin hair is an important part of my skincare routine and grooming. Stray hairs on your chin is unappealing, just as nose hairs sticking out your nostrils. Many women deal with chin hair. I have had conversations about this with my mom, sisters, and girlfriends. My concern was that my chin was looking and feeling bumpy and had dark spots. So, I use different products to lighten the dark spots and it's slowly working.

In 2017, I started exfoliating my chin, in circular motion, once a week with Tree Hut Shea Sugar Scrub Coconut Lime to tease out stubborn ingrown hairs. It really makes a difference. It leaves my chin feeling soft and the ingrown hair is easier to tweeze. I tweeze with Tweezerman Slant Tweezers; they are great and affordable. They are precise and do the job with very little effort. Over the years I've used many tweezers and this is by far the best one.

If you have excessive chin hair, you may want to consult with your doctor to make sure there is nothing serious going on. A variety of products and methods (inexpensive to very expensive) are available to remove facial hair, i.e., creams, shaving, tweezing, waxing, laser, epilation. As I mentioned before, you will want to research before using any of them to make sure it is the right one for you and they have no side effects. And again, depending on what you decide, timing is important.

Décolletage

Your décolletage needs some TLC too. Many products are designed specifically for the area under the chin and neck, advertised to lift and firm. Personally, I like keeping things simple so I was using Curél on my décolletage. But in 2019, I accidentally found InvisiCrepe Body Balm while on the internet and ordered it. It turned out to be a great product that has given me great results. Under my chin was getting a little saggy. When I started using this product, I immediately noticed that under my chin looked firm. I was like, wow, this product really works.

Neck to Toe

Everyday right after I shower with Dove Sensitive Skin and pat dry, I apply onto my damp skin, InvisiCrepe Body Balm to my décolletage and Curél Ultra Healing intensive lotion for extra dry, tight skin to the rest of my body right down to my toe. Curél is the best lotion I've ever used. Curél does exactly what it says it will do. Best results ever! It is the best thing that ever happened to my skin.

As I mentioned at the beginning, I have dry skin; it runs in my family. In 1999 when I moved to the U.S. with my husband and son, I continued using the Pond's Cold Cream, Vaseline Petroleum Jelly and baby oil mixture until one day I was in Walmart and noticed Curél and decided to buy and try. Curél is the dry skin miracle lotion! It really works. When I use it in the morning, it keeps my skin hydrated, moist and feeling great all day. Curél is the only skin lotion I use all year round. It works amazingly in the winter too.

I keep Curél on my desk at work. I lotion my hands when I get to work. I keep it accessible to anyone who needs lotion. My co-workers use it and love it.

Girlfriend, if you are not doing this, I encourage you to lotion your whole body from your neck right down to your toe. Make sure to lotion under your breast, butt area, and in between your toes which at times are neglected and gets dry and ashy.

Whatever method works for you, remove armpits and legs hair, and if you love wearing a bikini make sure to remove bikini line hair. Some women for medical reasons can't remove hair and some women choose not to. Hey, it's your body and you decide. To each her own!

Do you lotion your body from neck to toe? If you're not, it's time to start. As I mentioned before, creams and lotions have to be your best friend, especially as you age. Your skin will love to be hydrated and moisten, and you will feel the difference. And remember, dry and ashy skin is not a respecter of person and it's unattractive. Curél or any comparable body lotion of your preference will take care of dry and ashy skin.

Body Odor

Girlfriend, you not only want to feel and look beautiful in your body, you also want to smell clean, fresh, and beautiful in it. Good personal hygiene habits are important to make sure this happens. Just keeping it real. You can look beautiful and all that but if you have an unpleasant odor, that's a turn off. You have to take care of your body odor. Upfront, this is not about women who struggle with personal hygiene due to health conditions or seniors who are challenged with keeping up with their personal hygiene and need help.

Body odor is a sensitive topic, but we're going to talk about it here. How do you tell someone they have an odor? It's hard, awkward, and uncomfortable for both parties. Recently a friend told me that someone asked her to talk to a female co-worker about her body odor. How do you have that kind of conversation?

I've been around women with bad breath and unpleasant body odor and my first thought is, you mean to say, your spouse, significant other, parent, child, best friend has not talked to you about this issue? I know they know. And that's not right! If there is body odor issue, loved ones should be the ones having this conversation with their loved one, of course in the nicest, loving, sensitive, tactful way. Not an outsider, like a co-worker or supervisor.

I expect the closest person to me, my husband, to tell me if my breath stinks or if I have a body odor and not let me leave home every day smelling funky and have people holding their breaths around me or avoiding me and talking about me behind my back. Because people do talk. People feel uncomfortable and it negatively affects the work environment.

Women like going for walks during lunch, especially if it's a beautiful day. That's great! I'm all for that. It breaks up the workday and you get in your exercise. I get it. That's all good. But if you're going to do that, please make sure to clean up after. Don't just walk right back into the office and sit in your cube or in your office without cleaning up and interact with others like if you don't smell and think that's okay. Come on ladies! Your co-workers should not have to put up with this. I'm not saying all ladies do this, but I've seen it happen. I'm just keeping it real!

Here's the bottom line, good personal hygiene habits are important. As we go through the many body changes and phases, we must pay attention and stay on top of our personal hygiene because certain conditions may change our normal body scent. And as we get older, that also brings a different kind of body odor that we need to be mindful of.

With that said, make sure to wash every part of your body well, from head to toe, at least once a day, with emphasis on your armpits, underneath your breasts, belly button, private area, butt area (and in between), and in between your toes (and make sure to dry between toes properly to prevent fungus).

Use products to prevent bad breath, and underarm, vaginal, and foot odors. If whatever you use is doing the job, stick with it. If it's not, then find products that will do the job. Now, if odors persist, see a doctor to make sure you have no underlying health issues. Wear clean underwear and clean clothes every day.

After I shower I use Dove Powder deodorant and that works for me. I like smelling beautiful, so I put on mild scented perfumes. Chloé Eau Toilette

Spray for Women is what I put on when I'm going out. I've used it from the time I was in my early 20s, and I love the subtle flowery elegant fragrance. This feminine scent makes me smell beautiful. I've had people tell me, "You smell so good!" When I'm home I like to smell beautiful, so I put on Elizabeth Arden Green Tea Scent Spray. I love that this citrus aromatic fragrance is mild and fresh. Debora, my childhood girlfriend, gave it to me years ago and I've continued using it. These products work for me.

Some of these things may sound basic to some women but there are women with poor personal hygiene habits because they are lazy or not paying attention or don't care or just don't know better. Then there are women who struggle with personal hygiene due to all kinds of reasons, i.e., depression, anxiety and other conditions. These women know they have an issue and are embarrassed to talk about it or seek help. If you struggle with personal hygiene due to a mental or physical health conditions, please seek help. There are many trained professionals to help you. You will feel so much better. Please know that you are not alone. There are other women who are struggling too. Don't wait any longer, get the help you need, okay.

Also seniors, if you are having difficulties with keeping up with your personal hygiene, please ask for help. As my parents aged and realized that they could no longer do for themselves the simple things they use to do, it was hard for them to accept and hard for them to accept assistance. It was also hard for me to see them not be able to do the simple things they use to do. My siblings and I made sure our parents' hygiene needs were taken care of with safety, care, comfort and dignity. The truth is, many seniors are embarrassed to ask for help and that is understandable because it is hard to accept that you need help with simple hygiene tasks. So, if you have senior parents, grandparents, aunts and uncles, please ensure their personal hygiene needs are taken care of in a safe, compassionate, comforting and dignified way. You want your elderly loved ones to have good personal hygiene to avoid other health issues. One day, if we are not already there, we will be seniors too and should still want to smell beautiful from head to toe.

Are we good? Yes, we are! We got through this… Whew! I told you, we are talking about everything!

Nails

While living in Panama, I always had my fingernails done. In 2000, when living in the U.S., I had my first and last gel manicure because it damaged my fingernails to the point that nail polish does not stay on. Therefore, I stopped putting on nail polish. I clean up my own fingernails. I keep my fingernails short, same length and groomed. I have the best ever nail clippers set made by Ever Store that I ordered from Amazon. I also rub a small amount of Vaseline Petroleum Jelly on my nail bed and cuticles, especially in the winter.

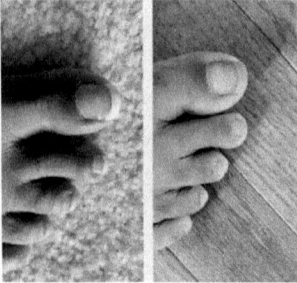

I go to the nail salon every couple of months for a pedicure and an extended foot massage. Jeny, my nail technician, gives the best foot massage. It is so relaxing. It feels like heaven! That's my "me time." I close my eyes and enjoy every bit of it.

During the winter, I don't put on nail polish on my toenails but as soon as spring comes around, I'm ready. I love my bold colors, especially hot pink. Sometimes I get designs on my big toenails and solid on the other toenails. However, I prefer the classic French design with white tip or any other color tip.

My salon visits are on hold due to COVID-19, but I look forward to "me time" again.

What about you? Do you do your own manicure and pedicure or do you go to the nail salon?

Heels

I have to bring up Winter 1999 again. It was my first winter and it was harsh. My worst winter experience ever! My heels cracked and bled; it was so painful. I never experienced anything like that. I could barely walk, and I didn't know what to do. I prayed to God and asked Him to tell me what to use to heal my heels. So, I went to CVS and saw Gold Bond Healing Therapeutic foot cream, triple action relief, and decided to buy and try.

When I got home, I applied the Gold Bond and Vaseline Petroleum Jelly on my entire feet and put on socks (to lock in moisture). The following day I noticed and felt a big difference—the cracks were healing. In a couple days, my cracked heels were healed. Ever since then, after I shower, I apply Gold Bond to my feet and add Vaseline Petroleum during the winter. I use Gold Bond all year round and have not had any more issues with my heels.

I can attest that Gold Bond Healing Therapeutic foot cream, triple action relief does exactly what it says it would do. I'm so thankful to God for this miracle cream.

Also, when I'm in the shower, I scrub my wet heels with a Foot Rasp File on the coarse side first and finish up with the fine side to remove dry skin and keep it smooth and soft between professional pedicures.

I love wearing sandals during the summer, so my feet need to look cute and beautiful. You got that right! No more dried cracked heels!

Do you have cracked heels? No need to suffer any longer, try Gold Bond Healing Therapeutic foot cream. I surely hope it works for you the same way it worked for me.

Deb's Just Can't Do Without Products

I shared with you my best beauty and total body care tips and the affordable products I have used over the years, some of them for a long time. I hope that what I've shared with you is helpful, gives you a boost, and brings out the beauty in you. A few of the products I mentioned I use all the time. Those are "My just can't do without products!" These products have proven to be effective and given the results as advertised and beyond.

Sometimes we wonder if the products really do what they say they will do. I'm here to tell you that from my personal experiences, these products have exceeded my expectations and I'm extremely pleased and satisfied with the results.

Here are my just can't do without products:

- Blistex Medicated Lip Ointment – lips
- Curél Ultra Healing intensive lotion for extra dry, tight skin – skin from neck to toe
- Gold Bond Healing Therapeutic foot cream – heels
- L'oreal Collagen – face
- Vaseline Petroleum Jelly – entire body go-to solution

I'm sure that over the years there are products you have been pleased and satisfied with, and you have your own "Just can't do without products." What's on your list?

Health Care

Healthy Body

I'm not trying to have an oh wow body. All I want is a healthy body to age beautifully and gracefully in and have a quality life. I want my body to be flexible and in good condition to take me around with little pain. Because as I age, I know that I'll have aches and pains, but the goal is to minimize them as much as possible. So, I'm doing everything in my power, with God's help, to make that possible. I do a combination of things towards my goal that I'll share with you.

Medical and Dental Care

Please, please make sure to get your annual medical and dental checkups; this is very important. This is preventive maintenance and early detection of any potential issues. You want to keep up with what's going on inside your body. The only way to know what's going on inside your body, is getting it checked by your doctor. If there is something going on, you want to nip it in the bud immediately. You want to find out early and get it taken care of before it becomes a serious issue.

I know women who avoid check-ups. I've heard some women say, "I don't want to know what's wrong with me. I'm afraid to find out. I don't want to hear bad news." Everything could be fine and that's good to know. Likewise, if there is something wrong, you want to know. The truth is, what you don't know, you can't fix. Please go find out if something is wrong and get it taken care of.

Many times, when you find out early, you can fix it and get rid of it. When you wait long then, unfortunately, sometimes it's too late. Just like a car needs checkups and maintenance to preserve it and for it to run smoothly so it doesn't break down or put your life at risk, the same concept applies to your body. The big difference is that you are more valuable than any car, no matter the brand.

Here's the bottom line: Your body needs to be checked and maintained so it can be at its best and function to its fullest potential in every phase of your life. So you can move around in it with confidence, ease and comfort. We want our bodies to be in the best possible condition for the longest possible time.

Know your body. Make sure you're in tune with your body and get proper and timely tune-ups. If something doesn't look or feel right, or you notice any change, go get it checked out. Don't be afraid. Don't take a long time trying to figure out what is wrong. Just go and get it checked and taken care of.

I keep up with all of my checkups (dental, physical, pap smears, mammograms, etc.). When I see or feel that something is not right, I don't waste time, I go and get it checked and taken care of.

- Are you keeping up with your checkups?
- When was the last time you went to the dentist or had a physical, pap-smear or mammogram?
- If you are fifty or over, have you had your colonoscopy? I did mine when I turned 50 years old.

Exercise

Oh yes, after age 30 or having a baby, it's hard to lose weight and keep it off. It's a struggle! It feels like your metabolism went on a long vacation and lost its way home. You're motivated to exercise and diet… and in some cases starve. Then you go on the scale and the numbers are still the same. It takes like forever to see results. You get frustrated, disappointed, and stop working out. Aww no! Please don't stop!

Even when you don't see the results on the scale, don't stop exercising. You've got to keep moving! Believe it or not, even when you don't see results on the scale, your body still benefits from exercising.

The health benefits outweigh the numbers you don't see on the scale. When you continue exercising, you will eventually see weight loss or feel it in your clothes (lose inches), slowly but surely. If you want your body to be healthy and last a long time for you to enjoy your life in it and have a good quality life as you age, you have to do some type of physical activity. You've got to move! Make exercise a part of your life and reap the health benefits.

As for me, I want to stay fit; that's one of the reasons why I work out. But to be honest, my real motivation is food. I love and enjoy eating. I like my desserts; that's the highlight of my day. I want to eat whatever I want to eat "con gusto" with enjoyment, if you know what I mean. I don't want to be restricted or feel like I can't eat this or that or feel guilty. That's why I don't do diets, just not my thing. But I do eat in moderation and practice portion control, especially now that I'm older and my metabolism has slowed down a lot.

I work out at least four to five days a week. I mix-up my work out routine because different exercises target different parts of the body. I stretch, lift light weights, combined with ab exercises and cardio. This workout routine works for me. It maintains my weight along with all the other health benefits that comes with it.

If you are not doing any type of physical activity, I strongly encourage you to find or tailor a fitness routine that works for you. Physical activity is so important, and its benefits are numerous (i.e., weight loss, increase energy levels, skin health, sleep better).

I'll share with you that in 2015 I gained a few pounds because I was not exercising regularly and my knees started hurting when I climbed the stairs and even to sit on the toilet. It got to the point I was considering replacing my toilet bowl to one that was taller to help with my knees. However, once I started exercising regularly again, the pain went away.

During the workweek, I'm up between 3:30 a.m. and 4 a.m. I have a one- to two-hour morning commute depending on traffic, and on the weekends I'm up by 6:30 a.m. I'm truly a morning person. In the mornings I'm full of energy with a clear and sharp mind, ready to go and do stuff. I like getting as much done in the morning, including working out. Because by noon I'm slowly and surely shutting down and by 7 p.m., I'm ready for bed if I'm not already in bed. Lol! So, working out during lunch or after work does not work for me. Due to COVID-19 I'm teleworking and don't have to get up that early, but I still get up early enough to work out.

Do you have an exercise routine? If yes, awesome! If no, why not? If you don't have a medical condition that prevents you from doing any type of physical activity, please find something to do. You will feel so much better. Consult with your doctor before starting any exercise program.

Deb's Exercise Routine

- Stretch

Stretching before and after exercising is important. I stretch before each exercise routine to maintain flexibility. If for some reason I don't stretch before exercising, which is rare, I feel the difference. It takes my body a while to loosen up.

- Arm Exercises with Dumbbells and Ab Crunches

As I get older, I find that I have less strength in my arms; therefore, I have to do something to strengthen them. I've always had a tummy but when I don't do anything, it gets bigger. So I do ab exercises to keep my tummy somewhat toned, not flat (that'll never happen). For these reasons, I do a combination of dumbbell exercises and ab crunches at least twice a week. It takes about 15 minutes.

Lifting weights build strength and tones muscles. With my 3 lbs. dumbbells in both hands, I do four different dumbbell curls (overhead, chest, biceps, triceps) at least two sets each, 20 repetitions each set.

Crunches help tighten and tone midsection. I do three types of abdominal crunches to keep my tummy under control and somewhat toned. I'm not trying to have a flat tummy, never have, never will. I love my little pouch! That's all me! I try to do crunches a couple times a week or when I remember.

The three crunches I alternate are: (1) Lying down elbow-to-knee crunch: three sets, 50 repetitions alternating sides, totaling 150 repetitions each side. (2) Standing elbow-to-knee crunch: three sets broken down 50, 30, 20 repetitions alternating sides, totaling 100 repetitions each side. (3) Standing straight leg crunch: three sets, 50 repetitions, totaling 150.

• Cardio Exercises

As we know, cardio helps burn calories and maintain a healthy body weight. It helps keep the stomach and hip area lean, which tend to be the problem areas for many women. I do cardio exercises not necessarily to lose weight but to maintain it. I'm at a comfortable healthy weight and I want to maintain it.

However, as I mentioned before, in 2015 when I was 53 years old, I was struggling with my weight. I gained quite a few pounds and could not get them off even though I was occasionally walking/running on the treadmill. It was like my metabolism went on an extended vacation. I was totally frustrated. So I prayed to God about it. I asked Him for help. God reminded me that when I was in my 20s, I liked riding the stationary bike. I was like, "God, I forgot all about that. I really liked riding the bike. Thanks for reminding me." Then I mentioned this to Carlos, my husband, and he said, "Sweetie, why not? Go for it!" So, I started looking for a stationary bike. I looked on quite a few bikes and read many reviews. It took me a while to find the perfect one for me.

Well, I finally found the perfect bike for me, the Sunny Health and Fitness Folding Recumbent bike and ordered from Walmart. It took me a month or so before I asked my son to assemble it. I had to get my mind right, if you know what I mean. My son assembled the bike in October 2015. Then in November, I got on the bike for 15 minutes. It was a rough ride and I'll tell you that was not a pretty sight. I thought I was going to pass out. Then I started questioning myself if this was a good decision. But I didn't give up. Every day I got on the bike and felt better and stayed longer on it.

Now I ride three to five days a week, at least 13 to 20 miles (between one and two-plus hours). I love my bike! It's so comfortable. I do all kinds of cool stuff while riding, such as pray, read my Bible, watch television, do stuff on my laptop (i.e., shop, write, pay bills, balance checkbook) and time flies. I don't even realize how long I'm on it. Also, I wear my sweat waist trimmer while I'm on my bike.

After I got my bike, I kind of stopped walking/running on my NordicTrack C2000 treadmill. We've had that treadmill for about 15 years. December 2018, I started back walking/running on my treadmill at least twice a week (approximately 70 minutes) because I realized that riding the bike and walking target different muscles in your body.

Whenever I don't walk for an extended period and start back, it's the most uncomfortable feeling. I don't like it. Moreover, walking is a good thing. I started thinking, when you are hospitalized and recovering the first thing they have you do is walk.

Once or twice a week I walk three miles and run one mile, total of four miles. While on the treadmill, I have hand grips in my hands that I squeeze together to build my hands strength. As I age, I've been losing grip in my hands, so this helps.

August 2020, I started walking outdoors with my husband once a week, on the weekend, for an hour, approximately three miles. We talk and laugh, say hello to walkers and runners that we meet along the way, and enjoy God's wondrous creation. Priceless!

Food

I enjoy eating so I eat what I like in moderation most times. I do try to eat healthy meals and eat no later than 5-6 p.m. I eat small portions and rarely go for seconds unless I'm at a buffet. As I mentioned before, I love my desserts and snacks, but I exercise self-control to control how often and how much I eat daily.

One of the first things I do in the morning is drink water to quench my thirst, break the fast, hydrate, startup my metabolism, and take my vitamins. When I go to work, I drink water again but after that, it all goes downhill because I just don't remember to drink water the rest of the day. I've been working from home since mid-March 2020 due to COVID-19 and my water intake has not improved. Once I start working, I totally forget to drink water.

During the week as part of my lunch I drink half cup of green tea or other teas; it gives me the pep I need to get through the afternoon. Then for dinner I drink a carbonated drink.

This year's game plan included drinking more water and eating fruits but so far no real improvement. I like apples and pears, but I can't eat them because they mess up my stomach. Right now, I'm only eating bananas. Oh well…

Recently, I had my physical and lab work. For the first time one of my numbers was off so I had to redo one of my labs. The nurse mentioned that perhaps I was dehydrated. I knew that was it because I was not drinking enough water. So before going to get my blood drawn again, I made a conscious effort

to drink more water and the results came back fine. I say this all the time, we are what we eat and drink or not eat and not drink. That's why we really need to watch our eating and drinking habits because it directly affects our health and the quality of our lives.

I had mentioned to Sandra (The Wig Boss) that I was having challenges remembering to drink water and told her what happened with my lab result. For Christmas she gifted me a HAIXIANG 32 oz Leakproof Free Drinking Water Bottle to help me out. I was pleasantly surprised. However, I still kept forgetting to drink water until one day I literally felt dehydrated and said, I need to drink water. On January 15, 2021, I used my water bottle for the first time. I drank every last drop of water. Wow! I don't know when was the last time I drank that much water in one day.

That is the best water bottle ever. I love it. I don't know what it is but there is just something about that water bottle that makes you want to drink the water. And to top it off, Michelle, whom I love like a daughter, introduced me to Liquid I.V. Hydration Multiplier (lemon lime), which I ordered from Amazon. I started adding it to my water and it taste so good. God's been telling me for years that I need to drink more water. He knew I needed help, so He sent me help. Thank you Lord! Woo hoo! I feel so much better.

What are you eating and drinking habits? Are they healthy? If not, are you planning to do anything about it?

Sleep

From the time I was in my teens I enjoyed sleeping and I still do. I believe in getting my beauty rest. As we all know, sleep is very important and has many health benefits. When I get a good night's sleep (six to eight hours) and I've not been woken up a lot by hot flashes, I feel refreshed, renewed, re-energized, 100 percent alert and I look great. Too, I have a long drive to work, so I really need to be well rested and alert.

I have girlfriends that have difficulty sleeping. How is your sleeping? Are you getting enough hours of sleep? If you are not, why? If you are having a hard time sleeping, have you shared this with your doctor?

Weight

Weight conversations are sensitive and personal, but because I care for you, we're going to have this conversation. This is about your health, the quality of your life, how you age, your mobility, getting around and moving around with the least discomfort and pain in your one and only body. Your weight plays an important part in all of this. Therefore, you want to have a healthy and comfortable weight.

You also want a healthy weight where you look healthy and good. Sometimes we lose too much weight and we don't look that great. I know this from personal experience. Previously, I mentioned that in 2015 I was struggling with losing weight and started riding my stationery bike. The rest of the story is that my metabolism spiked and I started losing weight like crazy.

Girl, I started fitting into clothes I couldn't fit into over 15 years and I was elated. On my 54th birthday I wore one of those dresses I could not fit into before and took a picture. When I saw myself in the photo I screamed! I looked terrible! I had lost too much weight. I asked my husband and son why they didn't tell me how bad I looked. They said that they knew I was healthy and that I'd bounce back. The truth is, they didn't want to hurt my feelings. I told them, hurt my feelings, I'll get over it. I prefer to know how others are seeing me, especially if I look bad so I can do something about it.

All the time I was looking in the mirror I thought I looked great. That's why I always tell people, if you want to know how you really look, take a full body photo. A photo will tell you the truth no one else wants to tell you. That was the lesson I learned. So, now when I want to know how I really look, I take a photo. I don't depend on anyone to tell me nor the mirror. If you haven't taken a photo lately, I recommend you do so. If you like what you see, great. If you don't, then you can certainly do something about it.

The other thing I learned is that I can't weigh at 58 years old what I weighed in my mid 20s or 30s and look healthy even though I am healthy. I'm about 25 pounds heavier than I was in my 20s. Although I'm eating better and I work out regularly, I've gradually gained weight over the years. I guess because of aging and my metabolism has slowed down. For my age, I'm at a healthy weight. I feel very good in my body and I look healthy and great. It's all about keeping that balance.

When you go to your annual check-ups and if your weight, whatever it is, is not causing any health issues, then good for you. But if your weight is the cause of any of your medical issues or would improve your health condition, then you really want to do something about it. I know women who because of their weight have knee problems, walk slowly, can hardly walk, have difficulties climbing stairs, sitting, getting up, are out of breath all the time, have diabetes, high blood pressure and the list goes on and on.

I know that when I go up a few pounds, I have difficulties climbing the stairs in my home and I'm out of breath when I get to the top, and my knees pain when I get on and off the toilet. I feel uncomfortable in my clothes because they don't fit the way I like. And I have a hard time losing the weight. It takes me forever to lose one pound when back in the day, in my 20s, 30s, I could shed weight easily.

So, be honest with yourself and the way you are feeling with your current weight. I know it is so hard for many of us to keep our weight under control especially after our 30s and after having children. And to lose weight is the hardest thing. You get discouraged and give up. I get it! Been there. But don't give up. Don't sit. Keep moving! It will take time, but you will feel better and you will eventually see the results. You are worth the sacrifice because, yes, working out is a sacrifice for many of us.

Weight is a personal thing and you know how you feel in your body. You know if you are healthy or not and you know your ailments. Your doctor can give you recommendations, but at the end of the day, you decide. This is your health, your life, and you have to live in your body. You have to live with your decisions and the benefits or consequences.

Please remember, everybody's body make-up is different; therefore, everybody's body weight will be different. Don't compare your weight with another woman's weight. The key here is, are you healthy and comfortable with your weight, in your body? If you are not, what are you going to do about it?

Whew! Another conversation that is never easy to have but we got through it. By now, I hope you know I care for you and want the best for you. I know you care for yourself and want the best for yourself too. So we're on the same page. We're good!

Be The Best You And Live Your Best Life

Keep It Simple, Relax and Enjoy Life

Hey, special lady! Keep it simple! I love simple. I always try to simplify things. When I have things on my mind, I go to God first and talk things over with Him. This is usually early morning when I wake up. While I'm thinking things through calmly, I'm also talking with God and asking Him to give me simple and practical solutions and ways to get things done the simplest and most efficient way. And I'm not talking about cutting corners or doing things half way. Because sometimes we drown in a glass of water and don't have to. Or make a mountain out of a molehill. Worry about small stuff. Complicate things more than they need to be.

Keeping things simple plays an important part in your stress level. We all get stressed about different things. I do my best, with God's help, to eliminate and/or reduce stressors. Too, stress can make you age faster and give you wrinkles. And I'm definitely not trying to precipitate any of that. If you know what I mean!

When I identify a stressor, the source or trigger, if I can eliminate it, you bet I will. If I can't, then if it's in my power, I reduce it and/or manage it to the best of my ability. If I need to seek help from family, friends or professional, I will. No shame here. Any available resources to help me get rid of or reduce stress, I'll gladly use. My bottom line is that I want to live a relaxing peaceful life. I want peace with God, inner peace, and peace with others. That is priceless. When you have peace, life is so much better, and you can really enjoy it.

"May the Lord bless you and protect you. May the Lord smile on you and be gracious to you. May the Lord show you his favor and give you his peace."

Numbers 6:24-26 (NLT)

"When people's lives please the Lord, even their enemies are at peace with them."

Proverbs 16:7 (NLT)

Sometimes you just have to unplug. You have to disconnect yourself from everybody and everything and find time and ways to relax. We think we can't unplug but we can. Once you do it, you'll want to keep doing it and wonder why you didn't do it sooner. Find and do things that relax you.

Take a "Happy Break" and have "Me Time." Pamper yourself! Find something that makes you laugh, that puts a smile on your face, that you totally enjoy, and makes you feel real good. Something that makes you forget your worries for a moment. And laugh! A good hearty laugh is healthy, and it feels so good.

What relaxes me and puts a big smile on my face? My top three are praying, talking with God, and reading my Bible. I also enjoy looking at my doll collection, which takes me back to when I use to play "dolly house" with my mom. And I enjoy long extended foot massages, facials, watching inspiring/uplifting/funny movies, listening to gospel music, and listening and dancing to R&B music amongst other things. These are things I do by myself and for myself. Also, I totally enjoy hanging out with my husband, my best friend, and doing relaxing and fun stuff with him. Occasionally our son joins us and we have a great time together.

Girl, the truth is, sometimes you just have to get away. Even if it's just sitting on your toilet seat, closing your eyes, and zoning out for a few minutes. Lol! Just doing that, when you open your eyes, you will feel refreshed and ready to go. It's just like people who take power naps or cat naps. All they need is a few minutes of shut-eye to feel pumped up and ready to go.

Let's talk…

- Are you keeping things simple? Think about what's going on in your life right now. Those things that worry you, that don't let you sleep at night. Have you explored every possible solution and options? Do you need help?

- Are you relaxed or stressed? Take a moment to think about what relaxes you and what stresses you and write them down.

- Think of ways to eliminate or reduce your stressors. Are the things that stress you in your control or out of your control? What can you do to eliminate, reduce, or manage your stressors? Do you think you need professional help?

- Find time and ways to relax. When was the last time you did something relaxing? How often do you do relaxing things? What are the things you enjoy that put a smile on your face and make you feel real good? Make sure to do relaxing things at least once a week. Take a "happy break" and get your "me time" in.

- Are you truly enjoying life? You have to! This is just one of those things you have to set your mind to do. If not, you will be miserable and unhappy most of the times. If you are a Christian, is your joy alive? Is the joy of the Lord in your heart? Are you content no matter your circumstances?

"Always be full of joy in the Lord. I say it again—rejoice!"

Philippians 4:4 (NLT)

"Not that I was ever in need, for I have learned how to be content with whatever I have. I know how to live on almost nothing or with everything. I have learned the secret of living in every situation, whether it is with a full stomach or empty, with plenty or little. For I can do everything through Christ, who gives me strength."

Philippians 4:11-13 (NLT)

"Always be joyful. Never stop praying."

1 Thessalonians 5:16-17 (NLT)

Love, Learn, and Live Your Best Life

〜⟳⟲〜

This is your time to love, learn, and live your best life. We don't know how long we're going to be here and in what mental, emotional and physical condition, so let's make the most and get the most out of our lives and our time right now.

Love

We have to talk about love again because love is that important. Love is the one thing that can bring us together and keep us together, no matter our differences. Love unites. Hate divides. Hands down, love is more powerful than hate. It defeats hate every time. When your heart is filled with love, you and everyone around you benefits. You will agree to disagree gracefully. And you and everyone will live in peace and harmony.

Love helps us deal with people and situations more calmly, with patience, tolerance, empathy, compassion, and sympathy. It makes us genuinely care for the wellbeing of others. And will never allow us to think of harming anyone, use derogatory words or commit violent, wicked, hateful or evil acts against our brothers and sisters. Love makes us treat all people with respect and dignity. It makes us feel good about ourselves and about others. Love makes things better, makes us better, and feel so much better.

To love and be loved is one of God's greatest gifts to us. Love is the gift that keeps on giving. It keeps us doing for ourselves and for others. Love keeps us going when the going gets tough. So, keep on loving yourself and others. Above all, keep on loving God, Jesus, and the Holy Spirit. Speak love and truth, not hate and lies. Be kind not hateful and be helpful not destructive.

Love can conquer anything and everything but it's a choice, your choice. You can choose to love or choose to hate. Choose love! Because love is the difference and makes a difference. If you want to be the best you and live your best life, then choose love. You will not go wrong, because love is always the right choice. Then you will be a true follower of Jesus because Jesus is love. Choose to love more and stop hate. It's time to show love!

"Hatred stirs up quarrels, but love makes up for all offenses."

Proverbs 10:12 (NLT)

"Love is patient and kind. Love is not jealous or boastful or proud or rude. It does not demand its own way. It is not irritable, and it keeps no record of being wronged. It does not rejoice about injustice but rejoices whenever the truth wins out. Love never gives up, never loses faith, is always hopeful, and endures through every circumstance."

1 Corinthians 13:4-7 (NLT)

"Above all, clothe yourself with love, which binds us all together in perfect harmony."

Colossians 3:14 (NLT)

"If we love our Christian brothers and sisters, it proves that we have passed from death to life. But a person who has no love is still dead. Anyone who

hates another brother or sister is really a murderer at heart. And you know that murderers don't have eternal life within them."

1 John 3:14-15 (NLT)

Learn

No matter our age, we never stop learning. There is always something new to learn. That's what keeps our minds functioning, growing, and youthful.

Life is not perfect. It is a mixed baggage of good and bad but you can surely learn from every experience, even the bad ones. We all make mistakes, poor decisions and bad choices. We are not perfect! We can't change the past, but we can certainly learn and grow from our mistakes and make sure to not repeat them and do better. Be always open, receptive and ready to learn. Don't resist it, embrace it. Learn, learn and never stop learning.

"Fear of the Lord is the foundation of true knowledge, but fools despise wisdom and discipline."

Proverbs 1:7 (NLT)

"Get wisdom, develop good judgment. Don't forget my words or turn away from them. Don't turn your back on wisdom, for she will protect you. Love her, and she will guard you. Getting wisdom is the wisest thing you can do! And whatever else you do, develop good judgment."

Proverbs 4:5-7 (NLT)

"As a dog returns to its vomit, so a fool repeats his foolishness."

Proverbs 26:11 (NLT)

Live Your Best Life

Love and learning are what we do through our lives. From the time we are born, we start loving and learning. These are two things we never stop doing. Both will influence the quality of your relationships and of your life. They are certainly an important part of living your best life. But at the end of the day, like everything else in life, living your best life is your choice. It sure is.

You can choose to live miserably or choose to live your best life no matter what. Because you know bad things are going to happen through your life, but don't let those bad things keep you down and determine how you live your life.

With God's help and a good attitude, you can overcome all things. Your attitude towards your circumstances matter and will make the difference. Sit down and talk to yourself about it. You can either rise and shine to the occasion and live your best life or be defeated and allow circumstances to get the best of you.

Choose to rise and shine in every situation. I know at times it's not easy, but this is when you need God's help. And through Jesus, He will help you. Be patient and trust God. Give things time to turn around for your good because they will and please know that things will get better with time. Just hang in there! Don't give in and don't give up. And while God is working things out for your good, because He is, He will keep your love, peace, joy, hope and faith strong. Always remember, God loves you, He is with you, and He wants the best for you!

God is the source of all the good things that happen in our lives. He blesses each one of us in many ways and different ways because we are just that special to Him. So, remember your blessings, all the amazing things that have happened in your life. Live your life to its fullest and enjoy and value every moment, every person and live your best life.

> *"I pray that God, the source of hope, will fill you completely with joy and peace because you trust him. Then you will overflow with confident hope through the power of the Holy Spirit."*
>
> *Romans 15:13 (NLT)*

"And we, who with unveiled faces all reflect the Lord's glory, are being transformed into his likeness with ever-increasing glory, which comes from the Lord, who is the Spirit."

2 Corinthians 3:18 (NIV)

"Every good and perfect gift is from above, coming down from the Father of the heavenly lights, who does not change like shifting shadows."

James 1:17 (NIV)

Be Always Thankful

We all have times we are not feeling thankful because we don't have the things we want and hoped for or because of bad experiences and bad breaks. But we should also remember all the good things and pleasant surprises that have happened that we didn't expect, ask for or dream of. And remember the people and things in our lives we sometimes take for granted, until we lose them.

I encourage you to take this time to think about all the good things that happened to you through your life. Think about the people who helped you in one way or another through your life.

When we take time to reflect, we will realize that there is always something or someone to be thankful for. When you focus on the good, the bad will be diminished. And even in bad situations, when you look closer, you will find something to be thankful for. Don't get me wrong. No one is thankful for bad things happening; however, there is something good you can find to be thankful in all circumstances.

A great place to start being thankful is by thanking God for sending His Son Jesus to die so you and I can live. Thank Jesus for loving us so much and doing what no one else could do. Thank God for His many blessings throughout your life, count them one by one. Thank God for loved ones and special people who have been there for you through thick and thin or made a positive difference in your life.

Having a thankful heart enriches the soul and spirit! Be always thankful!

"I will praise you, Lord, with all my heart; I will tell of all the marvelous things you have done."

Psalm 9:1 (NLT)

"Give thanks to the Lord and proclaim his greatness. Let the whole world know what he has done. Sing to him; yes, sing his praises. Tell everyone about his wonderful deeds."

Psalm 105:1-2 (NLT)

"Be thankful in all circumstances, for this is God's will for you who belong to Christ Jesus."

1 Thessalonians 5:18 (NLT)

Let the Best You Rise and Shine!

D ear fabulous lady! Please take care of your body, soul, and spirit and let the best you rise and shine every day. Do everything in your power, with God's help, to age healthfully, beautifully, and gracefully in your body, God's temple. And may your soul and spirit be healthy, beautiful, and graceful, bringing out the best you.

I pray that my best beauty and total body care tips, heartfelt devotionals, personal experiences, and testimony help the best you rise and shine—body, soul and spirit—all the way to heaven. I'm so excited for you! We are in this wonderful life journey together, and God our Father, Jesus our Lord and Savior, and the Holy Spirit are with us all the way and every step of the way.

Hey girl! Be amazing, attractive, awesome, beautiful, brave, caring, charming, cheerful, confident, compassionate, courageous, determined, dynamic, encouraged, empowered, fabulous, faithful, fearless, friendly, fun, gracious, grateful, gentle, great, good, happy, helpful, honest, hopeful, inspired, joyful, kind, loving, mindful, nice, patient, passionate, peaceful, polite, positive, productive, relaxed, resilient, respectful, strong, successful, sympathetic, thankful, thoughtful, truthful, uplifted, welcoming, wise, and wonderful!

Be all you can be and more. Rise and shine in your own way. Do you. Be you. Be your best version at any age.

Trust God! He's got your back!

> *"Commit everything you do to the Lord. Trust him, and he will help you. He will make your innocence radiate like the dawn, and the justice of your cause will shine like the noonday sun."*
>
> *Psalm 37:5-6 (NLT)*

> *"In the same way, let your light shine before men, that they may see your good deeds and praise your Father in heaven."*
>
> *Matthew 5:16 (NIV)*

BIG Thank You!

I'd like to take this time to say "BIG Thank You!" from my heart to your heart. Thank You for the privilege of your time and for allowing me to spend time with you. It was so much fun hanging out with you.

I sure hope you are feeling refreshed, revived, rejuvenated, and ready to be the "Best You and Live Your Best Life" here and now to be continued in heaven. And ready to make the most and get the most out of your life and your time.

Above all, I pray that if you didn't have a relationship with God, Jesus and the Holy, that you do now. And if you had one, I pray it is stronger than ever.

I sincerely wish you the very best God has for you and may He bless you abundantly in every area of your life.

Precious Lady, I hope to see you in heaven. But until then, I'd love to hear from you... know how you are doing. If you have a praise report and/or a prayer request, please send it my way. I'll be more than happy to celebrate with you, and/or pray for you and with you. Take care. —Deb

www.greaterisjesusinme.com

www.ingramcontent.com/pod-product-compliance
Lightning Source LLC
LaVergne TN
LVHW051411080426
835508LV00022B/3030